Henry Melvil Doak, A. T. Ramp

The Wagonauts abroad

Two Tours in the wild Mountains of Tennessee and North Carolina

Henry Melvil Doak, A. T. Ramp

The Wagonauts abroad
Two Tours in the wild Mountains of Tennessee and North Carolina

ISBN/EAN: 9783337146214

Printed in Europe, USA, Canada, Australia, Japan

Cover: Foto ©Andreas Hilbeck / pixelio.de

More available books at **www.hansebooks.com**

THE WAGONAUTS ABROAD.

TWO TOURS IN THE WILD MOUNTAINS OF TENNESSEE AND NORTH CAROLINA, MADE BY THREE KEGS, FOUR WAGONAUTS, AND A CANTEEN.

IN TWO PARTS.

BY A. T. RAMP.

EDITED BY H. M. DOAK, FROM THE JOURNAL OF THE WAGONAUTS

"Full of brownies and bogles is this buke."

NASHVILLE, TENN.:
SOUTHWESTERN PUBLISHING HOUSE.
1892.

Entered, according to Act of Congress, in the year 1892,
By H. M. DOAK,
In the Office of the Librarian of Congress, at Washington.

PRESS OF
BARBEE & SMITH, AGENTS,
PUBLISHING HOUSE OF THE M. E. CHURCH, SOUTH.
NASHVILLE, TENN.

DEDICATION.

Respectfully and Fervently Dedicated to Every
TRAVELLER
Who's a "Hell-ov-a-Tollar" Wherewith to Buy It.
By the Author,   A. T. Ramp.

> Some books are lies frae end to end,
> And some great lies were never penned;
> E'en ministers, they hae been kenned,
>   In holy rapture,
> A rousin' whid, at times, to vend,
>   An' nail 't wi' Scripture:
> But this that I'm a gaun to tell 's
> As true as that the deil 's in hell,
>   Or Nashville city;
> That e'er he nearer comes oursel'
>   'Sae muckle pity.

INTRODUCTION.

" Truth is mighty and will prevail."

THIS is a veritable chronicle of two genuine tours in the picturesque regions of mountainous North Carolina. The incidents, scenes, and descriptions are faithful and true, except where—for the benefit of the believe-alls and the doubt-alls—a note points out invention or exaggeration. The incidents are all veritable, although sometimes touched up and colored. The *dramatis personæ* is appended.

H. M. DOAK.

CONTENTS.

A thing of shreds and patches. ("Mikado.")

PAGE

MINUTES OF THE FIRST MEETING OF THE WAGO-
NAUTS—The Aliases Chosen................ 17

MINUTES OF THE LAST MEETING OF THE WAGO-
NAUTS—Veracious Chronicle................ 23

PART I.

DRAMATIS PERSONÆ........................ 29

CHAPTER I.

The Start—An Ancient Town—"Nola Chuckee Jack"—Bumpass Cove Furnace—The First Abolition Editor—The Devil's Looking-glass—Panier's First Poem—Luncheon—Ophidian Burnt Offerings—Grand Scenery—Titanic Battlefields—At the foot of Great Bald—Brutus' Thrilling Going to Bed—Asleep beneath Great Bald..................................... 31

CHAPTER II.

Brutus' Dreadful Awakening—Ascent of Great Bald—Botany—Grand Dome—The Hermit of Great Bald—His Ditch—Luncheon above the Clouds.................................... 46

CHAPTER III.

Snakes—Fish—A Mountaineer—A Mountain Ox Rig—Huckleberries on Big-Butt—A Noble Trout Stream—Hell-Hollow Fork—Fly Fishing—Accidents—Broken Bottle—Brutus' Crime and Trial—Cooking Trout—Finding Beauty Bothersome—Panier's Adventure with Snakes—Bardolph—Erwin, Supper and Rest........ 69

CHAPTER IV.

Unaka—Reminiscence of Ye Ancient Times—Platonic Admiration—Iron Mountain—The Killing Brutus—Meeting a Drummer—Commerce—Big Rock Creek—A Mountain Mill—Porte Crayon—Night—A Mountain Maiden—Emma Jean—We Leave Emma Jean Milking the Kine.................................. 84

CHAPTER V.

Ascent of the Roan—Fine Views—Arethusa—A Steep Road—A Mountain Grass Farm—Dining in the Clouds—Siesta in the Empyrean—At the Summit—Parting with Our Driver—Recollections of the Roan—Unchangeable as Ocean—The Brocken Spectre of the Roan—Nature above the Clouds—Science—Botany—Natural History—A Historical Reference..... 96

CHAPTER VI.

The Home of the Clouds—Cloud and Light Ef-

fects—Sunrise Rock—Valley and Mountain
Views—Big Black—Valley of East Tennessee
—Blue Ridge—Cumberland Mountains—Lion
Bluff—A Granite Sphinx of Nature's Carving
—Ruskin and George Eliot—Fooling Brutus
into a Walk—Departure from Roan—A Tramp
of Twelve Miles—Up-anchor for Home—Lost
—Luncheon with Beauty—Three Toddies—An
Olympian Banquet— Culture and Elegance
Dwelling in the Seclusion of the Roan's Base
—Brutus' Wife—He Resents Reference to that
Lady of the Imagination—"Six Miles and the
Demijohn Dry"—Caught Bathing by Mountain
Nymphs—Escape — Panier's Ducking — Umbrella on the Wrong Side—Roan Station—Suspected of Jumping the Hotel—End of the first
Wagonautic Expedition.................... 107

PART II.

DRAMATIS PERSONÆ........................ 133

CHAPTER I.

Knoxville—Recollections of Revolution — Gay
Street in 1861-65—Provision against Copperheads—Our Party—Our Turn-out and Stores
—Lorenzo and Jim—Summer Diversions—
Going by "Nola Chuckee Jack's" Road—Night
with Wagnerian Symphonies—Whippoorwill
and Bullfrog—I sing a "Caviare" from Trova-

tore—Jim Lies Down—Musical Resurrection—
Like Orpheus, I'm Followed by Jim—Fording
Big Pigeon in the Dark—Methodist Conference
—Pie for Supper—Chicken for Breakfast—Off
for Mt. Sterling—Up North Fork—Botany... 135

CHAPTER II.

Corn Scarce—A Surly Native—Cosby Creek—
Retail Liquor Dealing for Corn—Barred by
the Statute of Limitations—Camped in a
Spruce Pine Grove—An Old Church—A Fec-
und Region—Nature's Music—A Wild Camp
Scene—A Laced Cup—Spoiling Good Coffee
and Liquor—A Supper for the Gods—Jove's
Envy—He Thunders at Mortal Bliss—The Can-
teen—I'm Drenched—Astronomical Views—
Job's Coffin over the Side of a Canteen—
"Bethankit" Hummed by Panier—Night
Views—Memories of Camp Life—An Alham-
bra View—Boabdil—A Mountain Character—
Thespian Exercises by Camp Fire—An Aston-
ished Native—Beds of Asphodel, Fern, and
Spruce Boughs—Dreams—Night Noises—
Taking the Road—Revolt—Mutiny—Six
Bells—Rue for Grog—Rebellion Crushed—
Blanc's Narrow Escape from Poisoning—My
Botany—"I Jist Dunno"—A Wild Region—
Resisting Toll—State Line—Blanc wants to
Speak—Suppressed—Ups and Downs........ 144

CONTENTS. 11

CHAPTER III.

The Governor of North Carolina—Geology—
Dr. Safford—Value of Science—The Practical
class—Vicious Puns—Dr. Blanc's Great Work
for "Improved Punning"—Big Creek—Corn—
An Arkansas Traveller—A Native Matron—
A Coquettish Widow—"Ristocrats"—Snake
Bites, Past and Future—A Pretty Maiden—
The "Missionary"—A Little Girl's First View
of a Real African—Poetry under Difficulties
—Finding a Rhyme—I Drop into Poetry—An
Ode to Big Creek—I'm the Poet of Big Creek
—Ascending Mt. Sterling—Pulling Jim Up
—Cloud Views—Silence of the Summit—Thunderstorms—The Peoples of the Tennessee and
Carolina Slopes—Dialect—Chaucerian English, but No Dialect.......................... 160

CHAPTER IV.

A Good Man—Gathers Apples for His Mother-in-Law—Lovely Streams—Pastures Green—
Lizard Spring—Luncheon—Cataloochie—
Trout Fishing—Blanc Goes Gunning and Kills
a Copperhead—Swollen Streams—End of
Fishing—We Move On—A Suspicious Native
—The Keg Clears His Intellect—A Patriot—
"Ef I Lived in Groun'hog Hole, I'd Fight fur
It"—A Tar Heel, Who' Been at the "Crater"

—First View of Quoi-Ahna-Catoosa—Grand Mountain Views—Yankee Canteen—War Reminiscences—A Bumper—"I Hain't Got Nothing to Take Back Nuther"—A Confederate Reunion in the Mountains—Blanc Wants to Speak—Blanc, Unsportsmanlike, Buys Trout—Up Socoah—A Deacon—Trying to Invade a Church—Invoking the Christian Spirit with a Canteen—A Serpent—Blanc Ahead on Snakes—His Facility in Seeing Snakes—A Lovely Valley—The People—Log Cabins—Jabberwocks—Supper—Sleeping in a Church—Fleas Engaged in Calisthenics Down Panier's Bony Back.................................... 183

CHAPTER V.

Climbing to Socoah Gap—In Qualla—A Wonderful Valley—Wounded at Sunday Roadworking—Hauling Jim up Socoah—Jim Hornblower—Buying Corn with the Aid of the Canteen—Testing Drowning Bear's Reform—Reform Has Not Touched Jim Hornblower—Six Bells Promise of Corn—Mountain Poets—Wordsworth—Byron—How to View These Wilds—Alone—The Lonely, Solemn Raven—Engagement to Meet Jim Hornblower at Home—Lo's Portion—The Glorious Socoah Falls—Indian Traditions—Jim Hornblower Not at Home to Paleface—Indian Suspicion, Silence

CONTENTS. 13

and Solitude—A Signal Goes Down the Valley —Warned That We're Coming—Indian Agriculture—A Bashi-Bazouk—No Corn—Indians Drink Our Whiskey, but No Corn—Resolution upon Lo—Digging up the Hatchet—Risking Blanc—Disguising our Blond Brave—Young-Man-Afraid-His-Horse-Will-Die—Savage Battle — Picketus Africanus Scouting — Blanc's Polyglot Oath—Blanc Saved—Victory—Scalps —Laden Wampum Belts — The Schnicker-Schnee on duty—No Sunday Trout Fishing—Eating the Trout We Didn't Catch—Donning a Fiery Red Cravat, as a Lure for Indian Maidens—Indian Divine Worship—Corn at Last—Qualla Capital—Crossing Ocona-Luftee —View of an Indian School—A Strange Region 198

CHAPTER VI.

Qualla—Scorning the Useful—Deportation of Georgia Cherokees—Policy of North Carolina Grants to Her Indians—Part Stay—Drowning Bear's Reform—Its Lasting Effect—The Cherokees as Confederate Soldiers—Effect of the War—Cherokees Are Citizens—United States Guardianship — The School of the Friends—Indian Government—Scarcity of Corn—Calling on the Chief—A Very Intelligent Man—A Confederate Colonel—The Walking Stick

Brothers — O-To-na-U-la-na-us-tee — Old Indian Comrades — Jake Doyle and "Staff" — Jake's Mess — Loss of Tradition, Legend, and Folk Lore — Flattering Lo — Cherokee Language — Indian Names — Poverty of Their Speech — Panier's Dreadful Dilemma — Imprisoned with a Mountain Maiden — Narrow Escape of Panier and the Keg — The Bunghole — Leaving Qualla — Off for the Tuckeeseegee — What We've Seen — Lo at Work — Monday Morning — Bryson City — New Town — Stirring People — Industries — Mineral Weath — Timber — Hotels — Granites — Nantchala — Down the Little Tennessee..................................... 222

CHAPTER VII.

No Corn — A Starving Country — Bushnell — Jim — A Hospitable Rustic Family — Technically a Deserter — A Man Who Was at Petersburg — War Scenes — "I Come Home" — Sleeping in Bed and Wishing I Hadn't — Willow Fountain — A Tree That Meanly Yielded Water — Down Tuckeeseegee — North Carolina Roads — The Advanced Season Here — My Botany Still Questioned — Logging on the Little Tennessee — Loch Katrine — A Lovely Sunlit View — Trying to Describe a Scene for a Painter's Brush — A Titan Battle Ground — Dissolving Views — A God-forsaken Spot — A Hell's Half Acre —

Silence — Gathering Fear — A Nocturnal Game of "Hearts"—Interrupted by a Ghost—The Governor of North Carolina—Panier Speaks to Him—Panier and Blanc Really Accuse Me of Nightmare 243

CHAPTER VIII.

Leaving the Haunted House—Mile Posts—Indian Sign Boards—Rocky Point—Clearing Out Saw Logs—Meeting a Road-working Party—A Lazy Lout, Shooting at a Mark, Scares Panier Half to Death—A Lonely Cabin—A Native Woman and Trifling Husband—Beautiful Falls—Ascending Great Smoky—Bathing—Luncheon with Venison and Champagne in the Gap—Quoi-Ahna-Catoosa—Another Mutiny over Six Bells—Champagne to Quell Mutiny—Renewing Allegiance to Six Bells—Taking the Oath—Dining in the Gap—Ambrosia and Nectar—Venison, Champagne, and Perfecto Cigars—A Toll Gate and a Row—De(s)cent Entry into Tennessee—Dialect—A Remote Region—The Chief Writer of Dialect Stories—Cacograhphy Not Dialect—Night Journeyings Down Great Smoky—Wild Rockets—We Land in a Corn Field—Resolved Not to be Found in the Morning in a Cornfield with Two Empty Kegs—A Roadside Dance—A Poisonous Julep—Rounding Chilhowie—Supper and a Nap in a Fence Corner—Maryville—Panier's and Blanc's Obtuseness to Music—A Forgotten Epic—The Author of "Home, Sweet Home"—Farewell to Saltus Africanus and Jim—Dissolving View of Jim on a Hillside—Knoxville—Off for Home—The End of the Wagonautic Journeyings by Field and Wild 268

MINUTES OF THE FIRST MEETING OF THE WAGONAUTS.

> Ae night at e'en, a merry corps,
> O' randie gangrel bodies,
> In wag'naut quarters held the splore,
> They were four jolly laddies.
> Quaffing an' laughing
> They ranted an' they sang;
> Wi' jumping an' wi' thumping,
> The very rafters rang.   (Burns.)

AT an adjourned meeting of the Wagonauts, held pursuant to adjournment—"Hold on," objected White. "This being the first meeting, can't be met pursuant to adjournment"—present the President, H. M. Doak, Secretary R. L. Hoke, and G. H. Baskette and R. L. C. White, private Wagonauts—it was moved by White and seconded by Hoke that the Wagonauts spend two weeks this summer about the Great Bald and the Roan, and the trout streams thereabout, in the mountains of Northwestern North Carolina; and two weeks of next summer on the trout streams about the Quoi-Ahna-Catoosa, to-wit: the Cataloochie, the Ocona-Luftee, the Tuckee-see-gee, the Socoah, and the Nante-ha-la, in and near the Cherokee Reservation of Qualla, in Southwestern North Carolina.

At this point the proceedings were foully interrupted by the entrance of a black Hebe, with four schooners of beer and four portions of limberger cheese, which, not to speak it profanely, smelled like sheol, with an ancient, a noisome and sulphurous funk. The cheese was labeled "Teufelsdröckh's Best, Eldest, and Fragrantest."

It was determined, *nem. con.*, that the Wagonauts should wear aliases; White, alone, the chronic objector, interposing, "The apparel's rather thin even for July." In deference to White's delicacy—which is well grounded—to mention of aliases, it was agreed that members might wear such other apparel as they might deem fit, belly-bands alone being barred.

The Wagonauts then went into an election of aliases. Brutus nominated White to be R. Elsie Albus. "I object," shouted White. "I want al-buss-in,' I do, kept *sub rosâ*, and I don't want to be advertised to do all-bussin'. Besides," he further objected, "the tying of 'perfide' onto Albion has degraded the name —it's a reflection." These objections were allowed due weight, and White proposed that his alias might be "Lucus," which, he maintained, was a literal translation of White into the *latinus vulgus*. Panier objected that this would be a *lucus a non lucendo*—White wasn't lucid, and alba never lucus. "Let it be Blanc, then," suggested Hoke. "I'm not a blank cartridge," cried White, besides 'twould be profanity." "It's

MINUTES OF THE FIRST MEETING. 19

sweetly suggestive of blanc-mange. Cur-ious you hadn't observed that," suggested Baskette.

"Why not Candidatus to the Wagonautic roamin' uns?" suggested White. "Let me

> Be candidatus then and put it on
> And help to "put a head on" a headless Rome (roam)."

Doak objected that the Wagonauts wouldn't be headless roamers, or their expedition a headless roam, when he was to be Jason of the party.

It was agreed that, while perfide Alba was going too far, White and candidatus were not by any means synonymns. Panier went so far as to say that White didn't mean candid, which was ruled out as a reflection on Dr. White's Latin and "parts of speech."

The previous question was moved, and the question came on upon the motion to adopt Blanc, which was carried, so White will go as Dr. R. Elsie Blanc.

It was then moved that Baskette be clad in an alias composed of the French for "Basket," and "Corbeille" was moved. It was objected by Blanc that Corbeille is a basket in general, while we need a synonym for the particular wastebasket we're borrowing from the *Banner* editorial rooms. Brutus suggested that Panier is a waist basket. "Yes," said Baskette, "but it's worn only by ladies, and then only on the other side of the waist." "And," suggested Doak,

"Panier's a little basket; and there's no waste of little Baskettes about our friend's premises. Besides the lean and hungry Baskette's French enough now and waste enough too."

"If we could find something expressive of a bread basket or a champagne basket, it would be the very thing to express our friend," said Hoke.

The previous question was moved, and "Panier" unanimously carried as the alias of our waste Baskette.

Further proceedings were interrupted by the entrance of Hebe with further schooners, which were charged up to Blanc and the Club thus hit harmlessly by a —— charge.

The suggestion of Brutus as Mr. Hoke's alias was unanimously adopted, after the universal objector, Blanc, had assailed it with a poor effort at wit, that it was a Brute part to kill so capital a calf as Brutus was showing himself to be by his manner of sucking his schooner of beer, and then to make nothing better of him than Brutus. He thought it would im-Brut-us as a club. This stale calf joke of Lord Bacon was hamstrung on a peg, as one that couldn't be porked off on living Wagonauts.

It was then decided that the President and Jason of the expedition should go as A. T. Ramp. Panier, who by this time had grown maudlin, said that the title was a perfect fit, that our President was a natural tramp, a capital T-R-R-Ramp; he'd a ram(p)art in these things—he's a ram-part of strength. Brutus added: "A. T. Ramp would be the ram-part of anything he'd go-at." A. T. Ramp was then unanimously elected the historiographer of the expedition and bidden to be in all things truthful, and to set down naught in malice and, especially, to be gentle and forbearing towards the shortcomings and frailties of Blanc and Panier. He was directed to lay in all supplies and charge to the score of Blanc; but, upon no account, to allow Blanc to have the handling of fluid stores.

Suggestion of snakes having been entered upon the journal, Dr. R. Elsie Blanc was elected surgeon and medical purveyor in ordinary to the Jason of the expedition, who was, however, given the keys to the kegs. Dr. Blanc's long practice and experience in snakes was deemed as rather fitting him to deal with snakes after they'd been raised than to commend him as a person to have the keeping of the means of raising snakes. Dr. Blanc's views on the subject of snake remedies being well-known to the Wagonauts, the President was instructed to follow implicitly any directions of his as to the character of antidotes to be selected. Ramp was further instructed to be careful, as historiographer, to avoid exaggeration and invention and never to admit that there was anything he didn't know.

After another schooner, charged to Blanc, the Wagonauts cleaned up the savory fragments of Limberger, deodorized themselves with nickel cigars of the Mundungus brand, and adjourned *sine die*.

R. L. BRUTUS, *Secretary*.

MINUTES OF THE LAST MEETING OF THE WAGONAUTS.

Farewell, forever, fare thee well. (Othello.)
Be thou as chaste as ice, as pure as snow, thou shalt not escape calumny. (Hamlet.)

THE Wagonauts assembled pursuant to adjournment, A. T. Ramp in the chair. The Club met to read, consider, and approve the report of the President upon the First and Second Wagonautic Expeditions.

The Secretary cannot proceed without bestowing a line upon the scene. The portly, noble and venerable A. T. Ramp sits at the head of the table, his rotund, orbed, and moon-sphered face wreathed in smiles, and yet his attitude is one of conscious command and dignity. He gravely recognizes the responsibilities of his station, as he sits, as one on whom all the gods had set their seal to give the world assurance of a man. About him are ranged the companions of his late toil and glory. He is clad in the rapt spoils of the warpath. A gigantic headdress of eagles' plumes surmounts that noble brow—a fit and aspiring coiffure for that bald dome of thought and of rule which his friends have, not ineptly, named, "The Great Bald." A necklace of bears' claws is clasped about that brawny neck. As a coronet of honor and not for use, by his side is displayed a coonskin cap, whose tail dangles coquettishly down by the side of the tablecloth and tempts a litter of festive kittens to play, with confidence in the beaming good nature of that great man until they actually climb upon his shoulder and toy with that adamantine cheek, which has blanched the stern faces of foemen in mortal combat, and yet disdains not the playful toyings of gentle puss.

It was the spirit of a low envy that led Blanc to whisper it about that this coonskin was no hard-earned trophy, won from its savage possessor in honorable combat; but the ignoble pelt of a pet coon, slain by the accidental discharge of Ramp's fowling piece as he climbed a fence in fast and disgraceful retreat, in mortal fear of the harmless pet of Indian papooses.

Even the fair-seeming Panier has been heard to whisper that the bears' claws are the claws of a sacred stuffed bear, kept in the wigwam of the great Medicine Man of the Qualla-Quoi-Ahna-Catoosa, sacred to the mighty spirit of Gitche-Manitou, shot by Ramp, by pure accident, as he turned to flee from the dummy bear in mortal fear.

Let them hurl their shafts, barbed with envy and tinctured in the woora-woora of biting jealousy, upon vulnerable crests. The darts of envy fall harmless upon the head of our mighty hero, Ramrod and traveller, who hath encompassed so many lands.

From the wampum belt of the President dangle two glory scalps, torn from the ensanguined skulls of twin hostile braves, during the great battle of Soconh, where Ramp rescued Blanc and Panier from certain death, and enabled them to see the light of another day, and the opportunity to assail his fame with envy. Envy has not spared even these gory trophies of a hard-fought battle. Panier hath spread it abroad in low whispers that he detected Ramp, wandering, reeling along Gay Street, in Knoxville, the redoubtable hero filling himself up from the canteen with limberger courage, and finally assailing and scalping two Indian tobacco signs. Panier swears that he saw A. T. Ramp creep stealthily up to and tear the scalps from these peaceful Indians, wantonly hurl them in the gutter, and bespoil them of tomahawk and bended bow and quiver. Blanc has even been mean enough and blind enough to assail the archæology of Ramp, and to swear that one of the scalps is that of a friendly Scotch Highlander, ye lad in kilt, who was doing duty as a tobacco sign, and no Indian at all. Envy could go no further; traduction hath here wrought its worst.

The noble Ramp is secretly aware of these aspersions of envy; but, with the divine magnanimity of the man, he accepts a sycophantic lip-service and forgives.

As our noble President and late Jason rapped the house to order, four schooners of sparkling beer trembled invitingly upon the table, and the genial incense of four portions of limberger gratefully ascended upon the midnight air. The following proceedings were then had, to-wit:

1. *Resolved*, That the Wagonauts congratulate themselves and the public upon the happy ending of their two vast explorations, and especially their great leader upon his truthful report of the adventures of the Wagonauts in their quest for the golden fleece of unsuspecting Carolina lambs, and, themselves, that they have gone for wool and returned unshorn—brought back alive by their gallant leader—safe and sound, after all their perils. They congratulate themselves that they have been graciously permitted to be sharers in his hardships and in his glories.

2. That the Wagonauts gratefully adopt the veracious record of their wanderings as a verisimilitudinous history of their exploits; and, while they are not unmindful that their historiographer has taken all the best things said unto himself, and laid all the worst puns upon his comrades, made himself the center and hero of all the great deeds, and laid all the disgraceful doings upon his late comrades; yet, this is the course of history, and what we want is Simon Pure history.

3. That this faithful chronicle be printed at the expense of the public, or charged to Blanc.

After these flattering resolutions were adopted, our noble President arose, with tears and beer streaming down his manly nose, and dripping from his kindly chin and bedewing his ample cheek and said, choking with sobs: "Comrades, Wagonauts, sharers of my toils, my trials, my hardships, and my glory, I owe to all of you—except what you owe to me—as favor, protection, safety, honor, aye life itself —'owes me for four rounds of schooners and limberger,' whispered the envious Blanc—'and me for six,' whispered Panier—'which will never be paid,' chimed both in unison, with Thersitian speech—"a debt which I can never repay," continued Ramp. "And yet I feel that I have only done my duty," and he sat down sobbing as if his great heart would break, full of emotion and beer, and redolent of fragrant limberger, amid rounds of roof-shattering applause; and the last meeting of the Wagonauts adjourned *sine die*.

R. L. BRUTUS, *Secretary.*

PART FIRST.

THE BALD AND THE ROAN.

DRAMATIS PERSONÆ.

R. L. Hoke, A Critical Writer - - - - - *Brutus.*
G. H. Baskette, Editor *Nashville Banner* - *Gid H. Panier.*
H. M. Doak, Clerk U. S. Circuit Court - *A. T. Ramp.*

R. L. C. BLANC. BRUTUS.
G. H. PANIER. A. T. RAMP.

THE WAGONAUTS ABROAD.

CHAPTER I.

> The wagon cheered, Jonesboro cleared,
> Merrily did we drop,
> Below the hill, below the kirk,
> Below the courthouse top. (Coleridge.)

THE three wagonauts—R. L. Brutus, Gideon H. Panier, and A. T. Ramp, the historiographer of the wagonautic search for golden fun and the self-constituted Jason, quartermaster and commissary of the wagonautic expedition—reached the historic town of Jonesboro at 6 o'clock Monday morning. Panier and Brutus were given leave to gaze upon the architectural treasures of this, the oldest town in Tennessee, where Andrew Jackson held court and John Sevier—"Nola Chucky Jack"—entertained gaping crowds of admirers at street corners, while he rested from the hardships of the wild warpath. Jason stirred up a livery stable and a hotel, and by 8 o'clock the Wagonauts were on their way to the blue mountains, whose azure summits pierced the skies eight miles distant. Our equipment consisted of Ben, the driver, two strong roadsters, a stout two-seated wagon, fishing rods and lines, a book of trout flies, a box of provisions for a cruise of ten days, consisting of potted meats, boiled ham, beaten biscuits, cheese, coffee, sugar, pepper, salt, a coffee pot, tin cups, knives and forks, and a five-gallon demijohn of old rye as a preventive of snake bites, a corkscrew for drawing obstinate fish, a quart bottle wherein to store provision of snake medicine upon brief fishing jaunts away from the demijohn base of operations. As to the value of this kind of snake preventive, it is enough to say that, in a jaunt of two hundred miles in the worst serpent regions of North Carolina, our party failed to encounter a single snake more venomous than a water moccasin.

Passing southeast along the low Buffalo Ridge, through the old Cherokee county into the beautiful valley of the Nola Chuckee, we entered Bumpass Cove by an old metal road, which wound steeply along the clear, dashing Nola Chuckee, over high precipices, overlooking deep pools and roaring rapids. At a point opposite Embreeville we paused to gaze from a rugged backbone of a projecting rock upon the remains of the old village and of Blair's furnace, one of the oldest in the State, generally known as Bumpass Cove furnace. Below us lay broad, calm reaches of clear water, alternating with long, steep-down rapids, where the waters foamed and bubbled and roared and gleamed in the westering sunlight as they dashed down over great quartz and granite rocks, rough and rugged, or round and polished by ages of rolling and grinding of sand and pebbles. Below us, in the far, the bright river stretches out of sight behind a blue mountain. Beyond the river a broad valley-plain stretches to the outliers of Rich Mountain. On the river bank lay the old town of Embreeville, named for Elihu Embree, the founder of the first abolition newspaper in America, printed at Jonesboro, whose son, by the way, served in the Confederate army. At our feet the beautiful river, compressed to a few feet, rushed swiftly but calmly down a gorge cut through an immense sandstone rock, on the headland end of which we stood and surveyed the other end where it cropped sheer up out of the ground beyond the river, a huge backbone of forty feet in height. The river had once formed here a lake and a fall, until it cut its way through and around the end of the rock and went roaring and seething and hissing, flouting the angry, frowning rock and leaving it scowling, while the glad waters danced on their way to the ocean. So it has gone roaring and bubbling for many a day, and still

> It bubbles and seethes and it hisses and roars,
> As when fire is with water commixed and commingled;
> And the noise of its roaring to the welkin upsoars,
> And the flood hurries on never ending.

Behind us lay the valley of East Tennessee and the lovely vale of the Nola Chuckee, and around and before us blue mountains, from the thin-soiled low pine hills to the fertile beech, birch, and oak covered mountains.

Only eight miles from the railway and civilization we were entering a country of almost primeval wildness.

Winding along the Chuckee through a dense shade of hemlocks, laurels (rhododendron), ivy (kalmia) and dark pines, we came to the sparkling spring opposite the Devil's Looking-glass. The cool, clear water, perpetually bubbling like champagne with escaping gases, invited us to rest, and here we poured our first libation as a propitiatory offering to all surrounding snakes. The Devil's Looking-glass faced us across the river, a huge, perpendicular, frowning cliff, rising sheer eight hundred feet. Brutus admired himself in this truthful mirror and Ramp posed and smirked and gazed at himself. It failed to reflect the Apollo form of the wagonautic Jason.

Ramp here kindly recited for us his first poem, beginning

      A man stood on a frowning cliff;
        A dog stood by his side;
      The man leaped off the frowning cliff;
        The dog could had he tried.

A sweet, simple, touching poem, original in conception and excellent in execution, which has never been in print before. The change from the indefinite to the definite article is particularly fine. I recalled shooting a fine fish at this point thirty-one years ago, with a Sharp's rifle, while lunching at this spring. I tried to repeat the unsportsmanlike feat with a Smith & Wesson, and only failed because no fish appeared.

Leaving the Nola Chuckee here, we crossed over into the Limestone Cove, so called because of the occurrence of limestone, which is exceedingly rare in these mountains. A broad, fertile valley lay before us, enclosing in its centre the town of Erwin, county seat of Unicoi, which was first named Vanderbilt; but the old Commodore failing to respond, the name was changed to Erwin. Thence our course lay up the Nola Chuckee again to the Red Banks, where a primitive bridge has taken the place of the dangerous but picturesque ford of old times. While consulting a native about the crossing I spoke harshly of the bridge as an encroachment of civilization upon aboriginal wildness. The old fellow chuckled and said: "Stranger, you hain't agwyne to find that ar bridge as much civilization as you mout think. They hain't no civilization about hit 'cept the quarter you pays to git across."

Two miles above the bridge we left the river and began a steeper ascent, toiling up excellent mountain roads that wound up chestnut ridges, disclosing at every turn new beauties in the fertile valleys below and in peak upon peak, rising higher and bluer ahead. Sometimes our road, always ascending, stooped into deep valleys and skirted narrow gorges, lined with laurels and ivies, cucumber magnolias, dark green hollies, tall hemlocks, green undergrowths, and tangled vines. Through frequent openings in the green coverts of the gorges the waters of deep, clear pools lay dark and sullen in the shadows. Lovely cascades, roaring falls, and foaming rapids now showed a pale ghostly white and now gleamed bright and shimmering, where chance sunbeams pierced the gloom and fell in a golden shower down between rugged, rocky walls of deep gorges. It was a gorgeous country.

In such country rustic wit has it that daylight is brought down from the hilltops in troughs. Here and there we passed cabins perched upon rocky hillsides, where a few cleared acres showed patches of corn and of the fine tobacco now raised in this country, for the curing of which the natives have learned to build better barns than grace the tobacco regions of Middle Tennessee and Kentucky—better by far than the cabins they dwell in. Such hillside farms have suggested to the mountain wits that the "farms looks rolled up like, as if the settlers was agwyne to move."

Here at a turn in the road, high up on a steep mountain, opens before us a scene of rare loveliness. A cold, pure spring gushes out of the mountain side and runs across the road. A lofty peak, beautiful as "woody" Ida, towers above us to the right, green with broad-branched, waving chestnuts, whose tops and branch-tips are white with graceful blossoms. Below us and before us lies a broad valley dotted with white frame cottages and log cabins. That rare painter, the sun, is displaying his brilliant effects of light and shade upon green hills, upon the forests of purple peaks right at hand, upon the far, faint blue of distant mountains, upon overhanging bright clouds, upon waving corn, dark in the shadows of high mountains, or bright green in the full sunlight, and flashing back the emerald light like an army with waving banners, unsheathed swords and fixed bayonets; upon clear, winding brooks and broad mountain streams, dashing darkly in midday shadows over cool stones and around great white boulders or dark granite masses.

Yonder the noon sunlight gleams like gold, or shines afar a silvery white, as its beams fall at varying angles upon brook and stream, white stones and dark rock masses, or yonder on broad meadows of pale green timothy, fields of red clover, or waving acres of dark redtop, alternating with dark green maize and the yellow stubbles of reapen wheat fields.

On both sides of the broad vale lie steep

walls of densely wooded hills, with, here and there, bold, frowning cliffs, peering savagely out, or bare gray stones glaring in the sunlight. In the far distance tall peaks dare to lift their blue into the azure of the sky out of purple bases; and every peak is head-dressed with fantastic wreaths of fleecy clouds, that now float high and white, now blush and grow roseate, as if those grim peaks had whispered something naughty, now thicken, frown, grow dark and sweep across our point of view, veiling mountain and valley and dashing the faces of the hills with light, quick, grateful showers; then passing away, leaving blue peaks serene in clear air and forest and meadow, cornfield and stubble, smiling and reflecting a myriad hues, and gleaming with a million pearl and diamond raindrops.

There are many ways of ascent to the Great Bald, of which we chose that by way of the Flag Pond, so called, *lucus a non lucendo*, because there are neither flags nor ponds within fifty miles of it.

Pushing lazily on, half the time walking

in that delightful atmosphere, up our winding way, all the time ascending, although not without occasional descents into valley or gorge, we stopped at all the cabins and houses, interviewed all the men, women, and children we met, and found them, as I remembered them in my youth, obliging and communicative, but as incurious as savages. Along with abundant signs of progress and great personal improvement in manner, dress, and mode of living, these singular people still retain their mixture of native shrewdness, rare hospitality, and obliging dispositions.

One who goes through this country, misled by romances, to listen for dialect, will be disappointed. Brutus declared that they spoke better English than he was in the habit of using. Antique words, forms, and expressions, and the grammar and pronunciation of the illiterate may be found, but no dialect, scarcely even patois. "Spun-truck," for yarn or thread; " garden-truck," "truck-patch," garden "sass," "sparrowgrass," "settlement," with accent on the final syllable, "gwyne," for going, "fetch" for bring, "battlin'-stick" for the paddle with which the clothes are beaten in washing, one may hear. It would take the peculiarities of about five hundred people compressed into one character, to make one speaking such absurdities as the romancers manufacture. Indeed the speech of the native differs but little, scarcely at all, from the speech of the same classes in the lowlands of Middle and West Tennessee, and for the very good reason that these are continually recruited from the ranks of the mountaineers. Such was my recollection, based upon a youth of summers spent amongst these people, with whom I've played the fiddle, danced on puncheon floors, and hunted and fished. This jaunt has confirmed my recollection.

Late in the afternoon we began the ascent of the Bald's great slopes, outlying ridges and spurs, up deep, rocky gorges, every one threaded by its own roaring, foaming stream. Great gray or black masses of primitive rock rose up along the road and in the woods and occasional fields, looking as if

Deucalion and Pyrrha, doubtful of the soil here, had sown a double seeding of stones after the deluge.

A little after dark we reached the last house on the side of the Great Bald, two mountain miles from the summit. After some parleying and polite depreciation of fare and bedroom, and assurance that we could sleep with the dog in the porch or with the horses, or with the demijohn and the snakes outdoors, our host consented to take us in. After the fatigues of the day, with appetites whetted by the mountain air, and the odor of rye, poured out as a votive offering to snakes, we encompassed a large quantity of excellent mountain fare.

After supper our host told us that he had one spare room, which two of us could occupy, while the other might do the best he could in the family room, occupied by our host and hostess, a half dozen tow-headed children, and a comely mountain lassie of about seventeen summers. Panier and I at once moved into the spare room. It was Brutus's first mountain experience.

"There's yer bed, stranger; I reckon you're tired—been travellin' and maybe you'd like to lie down."

Brutus assured him that he was very sleepy. The fire burned brightly; the ladies sat with the bed in full view. Brutus stretched himself, yawned, and said he believed he'd go to bed. Nobody disputed this article of belief. Panier and I sat smoking on the porch, viewing our victim through the open door. Finally Brutus came out, and asked us how the devil he was going to get to bed, with those —— women sitting there in full view. I am sorry to say it, but truth compels me to say that Brutus left a full, large blank space before "women" in his remark to us. Panier suggested that he might undress outside and make a rush.

After paying his best respects to the demijohn, he returned, stood about the fire, yawned, and said he was tired and sleepy. Brutus is a man of desperate courage, but exceeding modesty. He kicked off his shoes, turned himself about the fire—as if he were spitted and bound to furnish an early roast

—until he got down to trousers and shirt in the way of denudation—if I may mention denude in nature. Panier reminded him that we had to make an early start in the morning, and that "early to bed and early to rise is the way to be healthy, wealthy, and wise."

I have never seen such gymnastics. Although he'd displayed an elaborately adorned nightgown, he leaped out of trousers and shirt, fell over a rocking-chair, indulged in a moment's Graeco-Roman wrestling match with the chair, turned a somersault over into the center of the vast feather bed, and doubled the cover over him, leaving his fancy nightgown spread out on the floor, and the rest of his apparel scattered from the fire to the bed, while the ladies sat dipping snuff, all unconscious that any one could be making all that fuss about going to bed. Panier and I sat chuckling on the porch, resolved that we'd see his uprising on the morrow. I reserve that and the ascent of the Great Bald for the next chapter.

N. B.—True, but slightly exaggerated.

CHAPTER II.

Upon a simmer Tuesday morn,
    When Nature's face is fair,
We walked forth to view the corn,
    An' snuff the caller air.
The risin' sun, o'er Nola moors,
    Wi' glorious light was glintin',
The hares were hirplin' down the fur's,
    The lavrocks they were chantin'
Fu' sweet that day.

IN the last chapter I left Brutus enveloped in one half of a feather bed, and modestly reposing upon the other half. When, as Cervantes would say, the rosy fingers of Aurora had streaked the eastern horizon with purple and gold, Panier and I arose from our feathery couch, and donned our apparel. The sun was over in North Carolina, and we lay under the shadow of the Great Bald, and beneath the canopy of gracefully curling mists, to which every dell and vale was sending its fleecy contribution. I entered the chamber where Brutus lay, clothed upon with slumber and modesty. Saluting the fair damsel, who stood twixt the fire and the table, with dimpled arms up to the elbow in a great basin of potential corndodger, I called: "Brutus, awake; shake off downy sleep, death's counterfeit; up; away."

Brutus awoke to the light of another morning, gazed upon the maiden, and said he thought he'd get up. The damsel went on kneading the mealy dough, her eyes fixed demurely upon the basin—went on kneading as serenely as, according to Coleridge, the lady, in the "Sorrows of Werther," went on "cutting bread and butter."

"I'm going to get up," said Brutus, sternly. After a pause, filled up with gazing at the dreadful light, streaming in from two open doors, at the firelight, casting the flickering shadow of the maiden upon the wall, and at the swaying form of the damsel, Brutus said, pleadingly: "I want to get up."

Not another sound was heard; the maiden neither blinked nor stirred, except that she that dodger stirred; nor sighed nor said a single word; the only thought came in her head was there to stand and duly knead that same panful of dodger bread, all mindless of poor Brutus's plight, as he lay there bewildered quite, with youthful modesty bedight.

At last one snowy foot stole from beneath the counterpane, a wild, fierce look of stubborn resolve replaced the modest mien; and with one bound he landed in the middle of the floor, pale but determined. Another leap and he was inside trousers and shoes, and flying down the rocky path to the brook below, and with him fled many a modest blush, a towel, and a cake of soap; while the maiden went on demurely kneading the dodger bread, innocently unconscious.*

After a delightful plunge into a clear, cold mountain pool, we stored away that same dodger bread on the inside, where it would do the most good, laid a sack of edibles upon the broad shoulders of Ben, and made Brutus chief bottle holder. A little of that old rye was deemed necessary—not that there

---

* True, but slightly colored.

are any snakes upon the Bald, for there are none; but there are snakes over in North Carolina, and none can know when they may start west to grow up with the country and meet the traveller unprovided.

It is a glorious summer morning. The mists are sailing high, scattered by morning sunbeams. The clouds have lifted from the top of the mountain and now hang high in the blue heavens. The woods are fragrant with sweet scents of birches, ferns, and moist smelling earth. Laughing streams, dashing down the mountain sides, or murmuring along their rocky beds in dark, laurel-fringed ravines, make the mountain musical. Great gray rocks, with round lichen eyes, loom up in the misty gloom of thick woods, like giants' tombs. Dark granites tower here and there in the gray, like frowning sentinels, guarding the sacred haunts of Titan kings.

Our way leads for a mile or more up a gentle slope, whose fertile soil has reared great wild cherry trees, giant linns, large maples, huge red birches; the graceful forms of the white birch, old oaks, walnut and chestnut trees, cucumber magnolias, and hollies, laurels, ivies, and the beautiful mountain dogwood, line the dashing streams, and familiar alders and elders still hold place.

Long, white spikes of rattleweed sit upon their tall, slender stems and nod to the mountain breeze. The magnificent foliage and showy bloom of the queen of the meadow is seen here and there. Spikenard, ginseng, angelica, snakeroot, bearsfoot, crowsfoot, and a thousand familiar plants and mosses, carpet with green the cool, damp, woodlands. Now and then a mountain boomer—a small, black squirrel—runs across the road or scales a tree. Chippy sparrows chirp, and snowbirds flit through the green leaves; but animal and bird life are rare at this elevation.

The ascent soon became very steep, and the trees gradually diminished in size, the air grew cooler, the woodlands moister, and now a fine spring invites to rest and libations. Up and up, and now we begin to see through the sparser timber higher points and sharper ridges. Plants and trees are thinning out, and new forms are taking the places of those that cannot endure the upper air. There's always room at the top, somebody said; but it's small comfort to those who can't reach or can't endure the top. The mountain ash, the birch, beech, and mountain dogwood are still constant.

The sickly, yellow green of the hellebore —gathered for making *veratrum viride*—begins to deck the mountain sides with its peculiar and striking blossoms of green in long racemes and irregular spikes, sucking poison from the damp fogs of the mountain. The hellebore now wears a baffled air, and a sea-green Robespierre sort of look of despair, as if it were bewailing that man has turned its poisons into medicine for human ills, where it would only kill.

And now we are in the beeches—grotesque, gnarled, stumpy dwarfs, that stand like gnomes, kobolds, and wizards, guarding with their weird forms places of enchantment. They look as if they might have been once little, queer, dwarf old men and women suddenly turned into beeches. With the exception of the red haw, the beeches are the last of the deciduous trees, and these shrink until, at the timber line, they are but miniature caricatures of the lowland broad, spreading beeches of Virgil, where, "tu, o Tytyre, dost practise a woodland lay upon the slender pipe." Above the timber line grow only firs and spruces, and such arctic trees; but none of these are found upon the Bald. Of animal life, here, where thirty years ago, I found wild turkey and pheasants, feeding upon the abundant grasshoppers, we saw only sparrows and snowbirds.

The Bald Mountain belongs to a, presumably, Col. Johnson, of Asheville, N. C., the Tennessee side, however, being in dispute. It is used for grazing purposes. Close grazing cuts the grass short and banishes the flowers, of which I once gathered here forty-six varieties. The State line runs across the centre of the Bald, marked by a stone, inscribed: "S. L., 1886."

The old ditch cut by Davy Greer is still to be plainly seen, although it has filled up almost a foot within thirty years. This curious mountain character came to the Great

Bald from Virginia early in this century. His appearance indicated Oriental origin and Virginia traditions, which followed him to the west, made him a half-breed Arabian, son of a roving nobleman. He took possession of the Bald, levied tribute like a feudal lord, grazed cattle, protected those who paid tribute, and waged war upon all who refused to recognize his right of suzerainty. For one of his murders he was arrested, tried, and acquitted on the plea of insanity. He was again arrested, escaped, and threatened the life of the sheriff; but the officer of the law was too quick for the outlaw. He shot and killed him.

This singular hermit ditched off several hundreds of acres of the bald top of the Great Bald and cultivated a portion of it, planting rye and potatoes, living in summer in a cave just below the timber line, and spending his winters in a cabin lower down, where he had a mill. I have often talked with Erwin about Davy Greer, whom he shot as he came down the mountain. He said it was shoot or be shot, and he preferred doing the shooting.

At a delightful spring in the edge of the Bald we built a huge fire and spitted and broiled chickens, poured out libations of snake juice, and spread a meal Virgil would have delighted to describe, in verse unprofaned by invasions of foul harpies.

This grand old mountain is innocent of house or wagon way and seldom trodden by the profane foot of the tourist. It stands here in almost primitive wildness, to delight the soul of the lover of undisturbed nature. It is not to be confounded with a Bald Mountain of the Blue Ridge, further east in North Carolina—a pigmy namesake, which posed a few years ago as a volcano. The Great Bald is a healthy adult, not given, like its molehill namesake to hives, or pains under the apron, or in need of paregoric, or soothing syrup. It is a staid, settled old mountain, of good, steady habits and fixed ways, spending its nights at home with its family of little mountains around it, and always up with the sun.

The views from the Great Bald mountain and valley—hill and river, farms and farmhouses, and the distant plains of East Tennessee—spread out like a map, are grand, and the sentiments inspired glorious; but there is a sublimer sentiment than these inspire. There is an awe-inspiring silence upon the ocean, when one stands upon the forecastle of a calm morning with one frail plank between poor mortality and fathomless gulfs beneath, and gazes at the limitless expanse of blue ocean and azure sky. There is an awful silence in the hush of bird and beast and all the voices of earth and air that goes before a storm in the deep recesses of a tropical forest upon a summer's night, when all nature seems to hold its breath, in dread anticipation, as the storm gathers.

To me there is a sublimer hush when I stand upon the Great Bald's green dome, with the overarching blue above, the haunts of men blue in the far distance below, and no voice of man, bird, beast, insect, or whispering summer breeze, to touch the ear of the appalled listener at that awful silence. Then one feels truly near to the vast Spirit of earth, air, and ocean, and feels His infinite vastness and his own infinite littleness. Then one feels like Faust when the earth-spirit came at his call and he stood face to face with a dread unknown.

After consultation to-day, at the hour of six bells, which is "Grogo," the world over, it was resolved that A. T. Ramp should write a genuine Italian sonnet to be read at six bells each day, beginning on the morrow.

Just below the summit, as we entered the timber-line fringe of dwarf beeches, our guide suggested a visit to a "wildcat still," which he said was kept by a desperate "moonshiner" down the mountain to our right.

"He'll take you-uns fer the 'revenues,' but I reckon I kin keep him from shootin'."

Out for adventure, here was a fine chance for a bit of diversion with a spice of danger. Concealing our tremors from the guide, with cold shivers creeping down our heroic backs, we turned off to the right and soon struck a blind trail, which led to the beginning of a brook, which flowed from a spring a few yards above us and went singing gleefully down a broad glade of open dwarf woods, which gradually grew into taller timber as we descended. The gentle slope which led us down for a half hour was covered with scattered granite blocks, that seemed to have been hewn for building, they were so square and regular; and some hewn for Titanic castle building, they were of such huge proportions.

Soon the glade narrowed into a gorge and the slope became precipitous, so that we had to pick our way down a rugged chasm, climbing from stone to stone, holding on by loose boulders or by the trunks of trees and saplings, or the gnarled roots and stems or laurels and ivy shrubs. The rock-bound gorge kept narrowing as we went; and the brook grew, by continual accessions of streamlets from either side, until it became a roaring, foaming torrent, where speckled trout leaped at roving flies, and darted back and forth through the crystal waves, flashing in the sunlight, tempting to sportsman whom time denied the privilege of casting a fly.

Not content with its steep-down descent, every few yards the stream descended some more precipitous rapids and ran, bubbling and boiling over and among great granite rocks, rough and rugged, to calmer reaches and peacefuller flowing, to pause on the brink of some wild chasm, upon the crest of some up-edged ledge, for a wild leap into the deep gorge below. We had to wade down the rapids, or to creep along the sides, clinging to ferns and ivies that scraggily grew along the edges of the torrent. The perilous descent of the falls was often only to be made by sheer climbing and clinging like cats to root, crag, and crevice and rough noses of sharp rocks. The falls were sometimes sheer-down leaps of fifty feet or more, making the descent very dangerous.

The views at the bottom amply repaid the toil and peril. Here, at the foot of a lovely fall, we halt and refresh the physical man from the canteen, stow away a biscuit or two with ham accompaniment, light our pipes and sit upon mossy roots of old hemlocks, beneath the dark shadows of tall spruces, that reach their giant arms into the upper air and sunlight. Overhead the rugged granite walls frown and lour, surrounding the great amphitheatrical basin upon three sides, and enclosing, as with rough arms, a lovely circular pool into which the foaming waters fall, with a roar that is ever to the "welkin up-soaring." We gaze upward at the white, bubbling sheet of water as it plunges over the ledge and down into the pool, at the dark rock walls, at the dripping escarpments and moist hollow depths behind the foaming sheet, at the fringes of graceful ferns upon the cliff edges, at the dark spruces and up into the clear serene blue and the yellow sunlight, basking upon the topmost boughs. The view is a reward worthy all toil and peril.

Further down we could see the stream gliding onward, for a space, peacefully and quietly, then bubbling and foaming down a steep rapids, to where it

Along the cliff to fall and pause and fall did seem,

for a flying leap over a steep ledge down into another rocky chasm. Over the ledge below us and above the crest of the fall, tall spruces lifted their dark tops and bathed their topmost boughs in the perpetual mist of the falling waters, and sparkled and glistened in the sweet sunlight.

"I see Jim's at work," said our guide, pointing out a thin smoke, curling up far down the valley.

Such succession of falls we clambered over and down until we sat and smoked and gazed in admiration at the wildest, ruggedest possible basin, encircling a vast pool, into which the stream leaped with a roar.

"Down that ar nex' slide we come to Jim's still," said our guide.

"How on earth does he get anything down there," I asked.

"Right down the way we come. Hit's the only way, er up the other way."

When we reached the crest of the next falls, we gazed down into the wild amphitheatre below, where we could see the curling smoke from Jim Brown's "still" fires rising up above the pine boughs.

After vainly waking the mountain echoes, until they reverberated along the rock walls and reëchoed among the crags above and along the valley in which we were imprisoned, our guide said: "I reckon Jim won't shoot without axin' who's comin'. Gone to sleep, I reckon. Some o' the boys wuz down last night, an' some gals an' a fiddle an' had a dance, an' Jim's wore out to-day."

"Does Jim dance?" asked Panier.

"You bet, Jim do dance."

We were ashamed to suggest our fears to the guide that Jim might make a somnambulistic assault and bring down two or three unoffending tourists for "revenues." We plucked up heart and clambered down the rocky pass, which one man could have defended against five hundred. When we were about half way down, clinging like wild cats to the steep sides, the crevices, crags, and laurels, a shrill voice cried: "Hold on thar; who's that?"

"Friends," shouted the guide.

"Friend, who? Don't you come down hyar. Stop, er I'll pump you full o' lead."

"Cyarnt I come?" said the guide.

"You kin come, Tom; but you jist stop them fellers right whar they is."

The guide descended, and after some parleying got permission for us to come down. A hale, hearty, ruddy-faced, good-natured old man of about sixty shook hands heartily and drew out a tin cup of "doublins," holding his rifle in the hollow of his arm.

"Now you're hyar, make yourselves at home."

As I looked at the ruddy, healthy mountaineer, quite a contrast with most of the thin, wiry fellows of the mountains, I asked him what he lived on.

"Moonshine an' middlin' an' corn bread."

Only his clear, calm gray eye bespoke the desperado he was reputed to be and his red hair the fierce temper he was credited with.

He pointed out his possessions, consisting of a worm "still," battered and bruised in encounters with the hated "revenues," a small mill for grinding corn and a number of mash tubs, baskets, a few old barrels, with "mash," "barm," "singlin's," and "doublin's" set far back beneath an overhanging granite cliff, which, with the overarching tree tops, formed perfect roof, shelter, and hiding place.

"Our guide says you can dance. You don't look old, but I wouldn't expect you to cut the pigeon wing."

"Jist danced all night las' night with the gals. That's how you-uns got down so nigh afore I seed you-uns. Hit's dangerous wakin' a sleepin' stiller."

He showed us the still and pointed out "dents" made by the "revenues."

"Two o' the fellers as done that ar bit o' dirt bit sand right whar they stood. When old Betsy talks somebody's got to drap."

"Did they attack you here?"

"They hain't never done that; nur never will, nuther. I hed her over to the cove, 'tother side o' the mounting, an' I moved her up hyar out'n the way like."

But the revenues did come, and he was taken and sent to jail, and to that I am indebted for the accompanying portrait.

Jim is said to have killed two "revenues" and three informers. He said to me, while in jail: "I don't meddle wi' the d—— revenues when they ain't a meddlin' wi' me; but I kills informers like snakes, wharever I finds 'em."

A MOONSHINER

Panier here indited an ode to the worm of the still, which I give:

THE WORM OF THE STILL.

Jim Brown's old corn and grist mill,
    By a dam site
Stood; and the be-dammed-up rill,
    By the mill site.
His gin mill stood beneath the hill,
    By a dam site,
Where crystal waters o'er granites spill,
    By the mill site,
Where spruces dark shut out the light,
    By a dam site.
Nor Jim allows, by day or night,
    By the mill site,
The hated foot of U. S. "revenues,"
    By a dam site,
To tread, with foot profane these avenues,
    By the mill site;
And, on the bank o' the crystal rill,
    By a dam site,
Where sate Jim Brown's raw whisky mill,
    By the mill site,
Crouched the dreadful worm o' the still,
    By a dam site,
And, smiling, spread seductive snares,
    By the mill site,

Prolific of head-splitting "tares,"
    By a dam site—
Sate smiling, with sensual charms bedight,
    By the mill site,
To dance and wassail to invite,
    By a dam site.
Beware, O mountain men, the siren
    By the mill site;
In hell a corner hot they're firin',
    By a dam site;
Beware, O mountain maid, the vixen,
    By the mill site;
In Hades a place for you they're fixin',
    By a dam site;
Beware, O Brown, the tempter
    By the mill site,
Or you'll yet be the sad preëmptor,
    By a dam site,
Of roasting room in nether hell,
    By a dam site,
For spreading here temptations fell,
    By the mill site,
For coiling here the worm o' the still,
    By the mill site,
Beneath the granites by the rill,
    By a dam site,
Beneath the spruce shades under the hill,
    By the mill site.

Panier's ode was received by Brutus with great applause. I foresaw trouble and an effort to oust my sonnets of their proper place, and kept silent.

Jim liked our lush better than his own beer or hot singlings and doublings. He apologized by saying that the boys had about cleaned him up last night, and no profit "nuther." As he seemed confidential and agreeable, I asked him what sort of "gals" came out to such place at night.

"Bless you, they don't come at night. Cyarnt git here o' nights. They comes out in the evenin' an' stays all night. As for gals, they're tip-top good gals. I reckon, maybe you'd not count 'em fer much in the settlements; an' they hain't got no character to talk up, but they're mighty good mountain gals."

After a parting tin cup from our canteen, we bade our host good-bye and set out down the gorge, a circuitous route of about five miles, to avoid going three miles back by the way we came; and a rougher, wilder, more picturesque gorge I have never seen, and three more wearied tourists never greeted supper and beds; but we were glad we had endured the hardships and dangers, and felt well repaid.

The next chapter will be devoted to snakes and fish.

CHAPTER III.

> Now safe the stately salmon sail
> An' trout be-dropped wi' crimson hail.
> (Burns.)

I PROMISED to give this chapter to snakes and fishes; but a moderate use of old rye has so exorcised the serpent that I might make a chapter on snakes as brief as that in the history of that country upon "snakes in Iceland." In the mountains one hears wonderful stories of snake dens, and mountain sides alive with rattlers. Upon my first mountain trip I encountered a huge rattlesnake, and since that time I have seen two dead ones. In many summers of fishing and hunting in the mountains of North Carolina and Tennessee I have encountered only three snakes, dead and alive. Our party saw no snakes. I am sorry for this; for I have always contended that nothing in literature exerts such wholesome moral influence as a good line of snake stories.

FISHERMAN'S LUCK.

Beginning with the sea serpent, in the loftier realms of literature, and coming down to the delicate subject of garter snakes—*honi soit qui mal y pense*—the discriminating student will find that the human fancy and the divine faculty of imagination owe more to snakes than to any other single agency. I need not dwell upon the first serpent. Where would man be—and woman too—without the first serpent? Brutus, who believes in the ideal, and eschews realism, agrees that no subject is more provocative of the ideal. Snake literature is pure. Even the garter snake may be dwelt upon and furnish themes for story and song, which will not bring the blush of shame to the cheek of maiden modesty.

We left the Great Bald bright and early for the south fork of Indian Creek, stopping for directions at Sams's Store—where we found the proprietor sunning himself in front of his own store. Mr. Sams is one of the characters of this region—a genial, jovial, obliging man, getting along without hurry, taking life as it comes, and managing to have it come easy, and yet gathering abundant gear and accumulating money, acres, stock, and children.

"We don't need doctors," said he; "our only need is for midwives, you can see for yourself." When Ben had got through monkeying with a refractory tap with a borrowed monkey wrench, we left the main road and wound through a deep, rocky canyon, over a very steep up and down road to a small church at the mouth of Rocky Fork, where we were advised to leave our wagon. A road cut winding up the steep ledges that overhung Rocky Fork, leading from the valleys above down to a mill near the mouth of the creek, tempted us to see where we could take a wagon, if we tried. No wheeled vehicle had ever been over it. By hanging Brutus and Panier on the upper side and pushing at the stern, with Ben using profanity and the whip, we managed to make about two miles of such road as no wagon ever ascended before. At one point we met a native coming down the hill with a bag of corn shipped aboard a small ox. The mill gearing of the ox was like the ox, unique. A breast rope tied to both bag ends kept the load from slipping backwards. It was girded under; and another rope, tied to both bag ends, was drawn about the steer's hind legs. The animal was steered by a rope run between his legs and tied to his horns. The bewildered animal had never seen a civilized wagon and three Christian gentlemen. It took the Wagonauts, Ben, and the ox-driver about an hour to get him by. When the driver got by he stopped and said. "You'uns is from the settlements, hain't you?"

We admitted that we came from settlements.

"'Pears like you come from towards the Butt. How's huckleberries sellin' over on the Big Butt?"

We were not able to deal with this commercial question in a way to conceal our profound ignorance, and we left him steering his ox down to the mill, wondering how three men came to be trusted out from home who didn't know the state of the huckleberry market on the Big Butt.

There is more idealization in fish than in any other subject. The theme doesn't compare with snakes in deep moral significance; but in the matter of the pure ideal fish beat all nature. I come to this subject with a painful sense of my own incapacity. I know not how I shall satisfy the multitude unless another miracle shall make a few small fishes go a long way.

Letting ourselves down to the creek, down steep cliffs, some two hundred feet, through laurels and ivies and clinging vines and over rough rocks, we whipped the stream for two or three hundred yards without a single "jump" of a trout. Reaching shady water, the sport began. I secured the first speckled beauty; Brutus followed; and Panier came last, and then beat us all fishing. Rocky Fork is a noted trout stream, and as rough as any I ever saw, not excepting the Hell Hollow Fork of Clark's Creek. Coming down at an angle of thirty degrees, it winds amongst great masses of granite and piles of drift logs, under a dense shade of giant hemlocks, or spruce pines, as they are called locally, in a deep, narrow gorge, whose steep walls rise high on both sides, their crests unseen in the dense vegetation. Its banks are lined with an almost impenetrable growth of gnarled, knotted, and interlaced laurel and ivy. It is labor, but labor that physics pain, to clamber over huge rocks, moss-grown, wet and slippery, to leap from round stone to sharp ledge, to poise oneself upon the crown of a smooth "biscuit" rock, looking for the next footing, to whip pools and rapids with the dancing fly, intensely eager and ever expectant for the leap of a trout.

These delights may be varied as some uncrossable pool, some unwadable reach, or some unscalable ledge blocks the way, chock-a-block, and drives the sportsman to drag himself and his rod through the tangled laurel. As Mr. Lincoln said: "This is about the kind of thing to be liked by people who like this kind of thing." I've always succeeded in believing that I like it; and Brutus and Panier were continually exclaiming: "O how we're enjoying ourselves!"

The brook trout is a slender, scaleless fish,

with huge mouth, dark back, and light sides, beautifully speckled with red and gold. In the ideal it weighs from two to four pounds. A dull realistic view reduces it in practical fishing to a quarter of a pound Troy. Whether it take the bait at the surface, or leap out of the water, or seize the bait in the water, it always darts at its prey. The sportsman uses an artificial fly, a grasshopper, a butterfly, dough, or a red worm, and an excellent bait at times is an insect, found at the bottom of streams, where it envelops itself in an armor of gravels, woven together by some viscous fluid, as an assurance that it is good for something to prey upon. Bait good at one hour is not attractive at another; and sometimes it is best to fish deep, at others merely to whip the surface. Generally the best time for trout fishing is before sunup and after sundown.

At six bells A. T. Ramp was called to read the promised sonnet, and read as follows:

To Mrs. Mary ———.

Ah! leave thy grief! Be merry, mine, to-night.
Love courses through my veins like fire-hued wine;

My heart's ablaze with ecstacy divine;
My fervid soul's aglow with rosy light.
The swallows southward take their mournful way;
But why should we go sad with wintry brow?
Let's snatch from care and chain the golden now,
And pluck life's budding blossoms while we may.
I know that envious Death rides on the blast;
And cold Decay lurks in the winter near—
Already Nature mourneth flower and leaf;
But Nature's quick'ning love can summer past
Call back, and clothe therewith the dying year;
And so my love shall burgeon on thy grief.

An active sportsman, beginning early and whipping two or three miles of good stream, should catch one or two hundred trout. Beginning at 10 o'clock, when it is hard to lure the trout from his lurking place, our joint catch was not above seventy-five, although we fished about four miles of rough water. After exhausting our allotted time, we enjoyed a plunge in a fine pool, topping off with a douche in a cascade, pouring down a smooth rock trough and polishing up with a libation to snakes by way of taking off the chill.

It is one of the commonest errors of human

judgment to flout the dangers of the road we have gone over. This mistake led Panier into an acrobatic exhibition over a pile of driftwood and down a ledge of smooth rocks, that would have done credit to a ground and lofty tumbler. Brutus was not content with bodily injuries of a sui-bruisal nature. Entrusted with the supply of snake medicine, he proved as untrustworthy as Judas with the bag. Poising himself upon the slippery edge of a huge rock for a leap into futurity, his foot slipped. O for inspiration for a poem upon the leaps that were never leapt! Brutus went sliding down the slippery face of the rock, holding fast, like grim death, to the sad neck of an unfortunate quart bottle. Coming up with a round turn at the bottom, careless of abrasions, he triumphantly held up the neck of the bottle, while the snake medicine went weeping down the obdurate side of that unsympathetic, uncheered rock, like oil down Aaron's wasteful beard. When consciousness of his crime overcame him, Brutus sank back with a lost look into the realm of things that were, and wept bitterly.

Panier and I bound him fast to a sapling hemlock and tried and convicted and sentenced him to be hanged, *suspendere per collem*, as the law hath it. The culprit meanly took advantage of his constitutional right of appeal from Philip as a convicting court to Philip in some other condition.

After letting our wagon down into the road, we made four or five miles of rough road and halted for dinner. Across the creek from the spring where we halted, a shapely sunbonnet, surmounting a comely form, beneath the eaves of a neat log cabin, led Brutus to undertake the preparation of the fish, to which I weakly yielded. After a long and hungry delay, Panier volunteered to see what was detaining Brutus. After a reasonable waiting for Panier, I instructed Ben to look after my fate in case I should fail to appear, and I went to look after Brutus and Panier. I had provided all that was necessary to fry a dish of trout to make Brillat-Savarin smack his lips, not neglecting a bottle of genuine olive oil. I found the trout cooked done, fried, and hardening to a crisp on a tray by the fire, an old woman at a spinning wheel and Brutus and Panier, surrounded by a dozen tow-headed children, plying a comely mountain damsel of about eighteen summers and flaxen hair, with all sorts of useless inquiries, having no reference to dinner that I could see.

None can ever know the trouble I have had on this trip with a weak and useless curiosity on the part of my companions, which is always coincident with a good-looking damsel. I find them continually addressing useless inquiries to maiden inexperience, when I want to be eating, sleeping, or moving.

Recurring to snakes, a sad thing happened to-day. Driving, pipe in mouth, after dinner, along the margin of a placid stream, Panier suddenly leaped from the wagon, exclaiming: "Ah! give me a weapon—a pistol, quick!"

Brutus handed him a pistol. Bang, bang —five shots rang out upon the still air.

"Another pistol, quick!" shouted Panier, as he danced along the bank of the creek, his eyes gleaming with eager and intense gaze into the clear water. Bang, bang.

"There, Ben," he shouted. Ben gave me the lines and leaped from the wagon. "There —under that rock, Ben!" Our driver seized a small fence rail and began vigorously poking about under the rocks, turning over boulders. Bang, bang. "There he is." "What is it, Mr. Pannel?" shouted Ben. "The biggest snake since the original serpent," cried Panier. Ben worked, groped, and sweated; Brutus reloaded the pistols; Panier banged away. After humoring for a full hour this tribute to the quality of our booze, which had thus magnified a small water moccasin, Brutus got down and took Panier firmly and resolutely by the arm, gently whispering: "Panier, there's nothing there." Panier turned upon him with a wild look of incredulous anger and—

"Yonder, see!" Bang. "Aha, there he goes. I've done him up."

Brutus led him gently to his seat, and we went sadly on our way.

N. B.—True, but very highly colored.

Our next stop was for the night at Erwin. While we were sitting in front of the tavern, a gentleman with a marvelous red nose—a nose that would have taken first prize at the promontory of noses, took a seat and began to make himself agreeable. "Isn't your name Bardolph," said Panier, with a cool glance at the vast red nose, and a fit reference to Fallstaff's red-nosed friend, of whose nose Dame Quickly said of the dying man: "A saw a flea on Bardolph's nose, an a thought it was a soul a burning in hell." For a moment Brutus and I sat, scarcely daring to breathe. Panier was tempting fate. The mountain man grew redder of nose and redder of face, and there stole over his brow an expression which meant: "This man's a guyin' of me; and ef he be, he's a dead man." Panier's coolness and the forbearance of his friends, who sat smileless, saved his life. A friendly expression came over the face of the nose, and its owner said: "No, my name's Squib; I'm puttin' up lightnin' rods." Not even that fitness of name, occupation, and nose with Panier's

Bardolphian misnomer could provoke a smile on the part of Panier's anxious friends.

I might describe the supper, the biscuits, the corn dodger, beefsteak, the hot-mush feather beds, which are yet allowed to torture human beings in remote spots; but I forbear. Night's ebon pall overspreads the rotund earth; mountain and valley are leveled and made one hue by thick darkness; clouds obscure Diana's pure rays; Panier is writhing with nightmare, wrestling with serpents; Brutus snores. In that condition I leave them until the next chapter.

CHAPTER IV.

*A mountain maiden, very fair,
Buxom, blythe, and debonaire.*

THERE are several ways to the Roan Mountain, the easiest being to Roan Station, Johnson County, Tenn., and thence by carriage to Cloudland, on the summit. Five wagon ways ascend the mountain—two on the Tennessee and three on the Carolina side. The Wagonauts chose a winding jaunt around through the Carolina mountains and a picturesque and difficult ascent on the Carolina side. Our way led up Limestone Cove, through a broad valley by the side of North Indian Creek, a broad, clear, beautiful stream, fringed with elders and laurels. Yellow stubbles, meadows, and cornfields stretch on either side to the Blue Mountains, which wall in the cove from the big world outside and cut off here a wide, fertile, happy valley, which needs only transportation to make it the home of a prosperous community.

Before us and to our right rises the long, whale-backed ridge of the Unaka Mountain —very like a whale and bare in patches, with what are called "huckleberry balds," which differ from the balds that lie above the timber line. Unaka, or Unicoi, is a generic term generally applied to a range of mountains, but here fastened upon a single peak.

Rattling along over a level road, we entered a long lane. We had lifted up our voices in song, when memory suddenly brought up recollections of my last visit to this region. A cool twilight scene came back as vividly as if it had been yesterday. My father, my younger brother, and myself rode along this very lane, beguiling the loneliness of the dusk with song. The past beyond the gulf of war came back in clear outlines—not with grief, not with bitterness, but with that quiet sadness of mingled sorrow and pleasure that lies so hazily blue in the past, with shadows sweetly tempered by genial sunlight. Two of those voices are forever silent for this world. My voice was hushed and our song came to an end. I sat for a mile lost in revery—a fabric of mingled woof and warp, of dark and bright threads, woven by the marvelous shuttle of memory upon time's wonderful loom.

Passing by the northwest end of the Unaka, leaving it to our right and rear, we began to ascend, winding up steep hillsides. Valley farms became hillside fields, hills grew to mountains, and soon we were upon the wooded slopes of Iron Mountain. After winding upward for miles, a turn in the road, in Iron Mountain Gap, brought us in full view of the Roan, with its dark spruce and fir crowned bluffs, its heavily wooded slopes and bold cliffs of a thousand sheer feet or more of towering rock. Cloud-crowned, this grandest of all mountains stood dwarfing all surrounding peaks. Between us and the Roan lay a lovely valley, with many a hill and hollow, whose myriad streams were sending up each its contribution of fleecy mist, to climb the mountain sides and join the grey nubia that hung over the Roan.

A view nigher at hand called for a moment's Platonic admiration—perhaps Plutonic in the glowing breast of the gushing Brutus. Two robust, handsome mountain girls, conscious of their own charms, sat in the door of a cabin by the roadside, smiling at each other and for Brutus and his dark moustache. The mists gathered about as Panier and I gazed at the glorious mountain scene and Brutus camped his soft eye upon the nigher view. Fine rain began to fall, shutting out all but the near view. Brutus thought it would be wise to seek shelter in the cabin, and expressed great concern for Panier's health. In the interest of a lowland maiden, we ordered Ben to drive on. Fortunately for him, Brutus's impressible heart is very soft and like the flesh of the fellow who was "stobbed" nineteen times and six to the "holler" at Napoleon, Ark., who said: "Stranger, look after them fellows I've been a ventilatin'; I've got powerful healin' flesh." But, alas! although his wounds heal by first intention, what enduring pangs he must leave behind as that dark moustache, far-gone smile, and Hamletic eye career through the country.

Secured against the gentle rain, which we

found only a pleasing variety, during the only half day that we had rain, we rolled on down the Carolina slope of Iron Mountain, meeting upon the way a solitary commercial traveler, sitting in lonely grandeur amongst his vast trunks and boxes. He gazed ahead, without so much as a curious glance, as Ben and his driver saluted. He reminded one of Eothen's account of meeting a British countryman seated upon his camel on the great desert between Palestine and Cairo, when the two exclusive Britons passed each other within twenty feet and merely touched caps.

The drummer is usually a genial fellow, full of a ready humanity. He is, moreover, the most abused of men, in view of the actual sins he commits. In general he is a thorough business man, a man of the world, a pioneer of commerce, the right arm of business centers, a blessing to remote regions, and a civilizing agent, whom a small percentage of the unworthy have given a bad name. We found that the ubiquitous drummer, with his feminine array of trunks and boxes, had threaded and raided, every pig-path in the mountain regions. We heard of him everywhere. Indeed, we found that sweet recollections of engaging commercial travellers lingering in the bosoms of mountain maidens were almost the only antidote to the taking charms of Brutus.

On the far slopes of Iron Mountain we halted under a broad-branched tree, secure from the fine-spun rain, by the side of a bubbling spring, and enjoyed our midday meal, with snake preventive accompaniment. Persons have been known to imbibe embryo serpents with crude unqualified water.

When the duties of six bells had been duly discharged and the canteen had retired with a clear conscience of duty well performed, A. T. Ramp was loudly called by the impatient Wagonauts to read his promised sonnet, which he did, as follows:

To a Lily of the Valley.

Ah! love! this gladsome night of leafy June
Invites us twain, with balmy bud and flower,
To linger late in fragrant summer bower,
Basked in the chequered light of harvest moon,

Where Dian lifts her amber plenilune:
More witching far, of night, this grateful hour,
That dewy sheen and star-gleam richly dower,
Than, in its glorious glow, the garish noon.
Ah! softly throbs thy gentle heart 'gainst mine—
(And leanest thou on me with perfect faith?)
Nor recks the rude impulse from mine to thine—
Ah! love! a horrid thought my soul affraith!
Oh God!!!—Dost thou against my heart incline?
Or, death in life! do I enfold thy wraith.

Now we go rolling down Big Rock Creek, our road winding along the edge of a rocky gorge, deep down in which the wild stream boiled and foamed, a series of deep pools, swift, smooth reaches, roaring cataracts, hissing cascades, and rough rapids, with green fields and meadows rising high upon the hills on either side. Here and there some quaint old mill, of a kind found only in the mountains, and of a type as old as settlements in these valleys, sat deep down in the rocky gorge, with wheel something after the turbine pattern, and arrangement with reference to the water, and an upright, perpendicular shaft conveying the power to the buhrs. Now an old and now a new sawmill occupied the post of honor by a dam site, and piles of pine, hemlock, maple, and wild cherry lumber showed the importance of the lumber trade.

The huge Roan Mountain now hung over us, with its sheer granite cliffs, its woody sides, and its dark crown of balsams. Choosing the Little Rock Creek road as the worst, the roughest, and likely to be the most picturesque, we turned to the right, crossing a high ridge into Little Rock Creek Valley, and began the actual ascent of the mountain whose sides we had been flanking cross-ridgewise. To our right, as we wound up the creek valley, I recognized the old Briggs house, whence I made the ascent in 1856. It was here that Porte Crayon stopped about thirty years ago. Poor Strother! the skillful hand that penned the finest travel sketches written since "Eothen" somehow lost its cunning when the author became an office-holder and allowed his literary connections to set him squarely against his own people in their death struggle. Aside from the issues and results of the struggle, the highest patriotism at last roots deeply and clings closely and tenderly in the sweet soil upon one's own spring branch. By all means let a man expand and broaden, if he expand with him a profound feeling that his own hollow is the sweetest spot on earth. No other sentiment ever wrought any good or enduring thing.

It was growing dark when the Wagonauts bethought them that they must stop somewhere, unless they meant to seek lodging with broken bones down some deep gorge. A small room in the rear of a new frame house, roofed and floored, but unweatherboarded, loomed up dimly in the misty twilight. Vague forms peered out from between the naked studdings. "Gentleman," I said, "here's our last chance; we must put our best foot foremost. One must go in who can inspire confidence." I went.

"Is the gentleman of the house at home?" I asked.

A sweet voice replied: "My father and mother have gone to the upper farm to save the grass."

I hardly expected to stay under the circumstances, and asked the way to the next house; but I explained that we were belated and likely to break our necks if we tried the road further.

"If you can put up with what I have, you can stay here," she replied.

Feeling that we were on probation, we brought in our movables, carefully keeping the demijohn shady, lest we might alarm our fair hostess. Emma Jean went about our evening meal and Minnie washed the dishes and set the table. In a half hour we sat down to a table graced with clean table cloth; brightly polished China and glass, and smoking egg-bread, broiled ham, coffee, fresh eggs, sweet butter, and fresh buttermilk tempted to gluttony. The demijohn sat and looked on reproachfully, untapped, and no empty demijohn ever looked upon a thirstier party of Wagonauts; but we deemed it our duty, as gentlemen, to avoid giving our fair hostess alarm.

Supper over, Emma Jean tidied up the little room, remade the beds, and then modestly, with the air of a well-bred lady, said,

"Gentlemen, you can sleep here; good night," and she, with the children, retired to a log cabin some two hundred yards away, as fearless here alone with two small children, in a deep mountain gorge, upon a rainy night, with three strangers, as if a company of knights mounted guard about her couch.

Canova should have seen Emma Jean before he carved his lovely Hebe. She was about seventeen, lithe, lissom, and exquisitely formed, with light-brown hair, fair complexion, sweet but firm blue eyes, that looked modestly but confidently, small hands, and delicate feet encased in neatly fitting shoes. Moreover she was ready, bright, and perfectly self-possessed, modest in *mien*, delicate in speech, and sweet-voiced. This is no fancy sketch of our hostess; but it is not to be taken as a description of the typical mountain maiden. Such women are rare in this region. In a latter-day Southern novel of the mountains she would figure as something lovely in face and form, speaking Hottentot.

We left Emma Jean with lingering parting, prompted by genuine admiration for womanly sweetness, modesty, and frank independence, and wound slowly up the valley, gazing at her vanishing form as she moved, pail in hand, amongst the cows. The sun was shining brightly as we began the ascent of the Roan, which I reserve for the next chapter.

CHAPTER V.

"Up—idee." (Longfellow.)

TO the tourist who knows that fun is a relative thing and enjoyment an imaginary state of the mind, donned as one puts on a coat, as often in rugged wilds and desert places as in gilded *salons*, I commend the Glen Air ascent of the Roan. Its views are finer, its ascents steeper, its hardships greater. A hundred brooks coming down into Little Rock Creek from both sides of the valley invite the tourist to stay awhile and whip a mile or so of noisy, tumultuous waters and then to find rest sweeter in his wagon seat. The best sport we have had was found in a stream one could step across.

After winding far to the right and as far to the left, we look down upon our road a thousand feet beneath us, where sweet farmhouses nestle in green orchards and fresh meadows stretch far away down the valley. The winding creek is seen far below, foaming over rough granite ledges, pausing to turn a thrifty sawmill or to grind a meager grist for a waiting mill boy. Yonder the dark granite jaws of its deep gorge open to swallow some gentle brook that laughs and dances down some flowery dell, flashing in the sunlight, as youthful maiden glee dances into and is swallowed by matrimony. Yonder, between two steep ridges, enclosing a narrow vale, we can see almost the full length of a laughing brook, from source to mouth, gleaming in the sunlight, as

> Arethusa arose
> From her couch of snows
> In the Acroceraunian mountains—
> From cloud and from crag
> With many a jag,
> Shepherding her bright fountains.

Now the road grows steep and craggy as we rise to the backbone of some bold ridge, and walk and push and scotch and "blow" our good team of smoking horses. Our ascent is a going to and fro and up and down, across steep ridges and deep glens, drained by tempting trout brooks. Now a lovely grass farm opens up on our way, lying high up on the Roan, with the finest meadows of redtop and timothy and excellent houses and outhouses. From this point we can see, in a gap above the timber line, the bald ridge of the Roan's indented backbone; and, descending some hundreds of yards, the great tramway built by some adventurous speculator, upon which to draw up hundreds of tons of wild cherry to the summit of the Roan, whence it was carried by a tramway of twelve miles down the Tennessee side to Roan Mountain Station and shipped thence to Boston.

Another steep climb and a turn in the road discloses a clear cool spring and a huge granite rock for a dining table. Snake medicine, old ham, ox tongue, beaten biscuit, corned beef, anchovy-stuffed olives, and water as clear as ever highest cloud distilled upon loftiest mountain's brow, to be rectified by sparkling mica sands and run over cool, mossy stones, for the qualification of old rye, invited the tired Wagonauts to dinner and repose.

THE WAGONAUTS ABROAD. 99

After the hands upon the dial had marked six bells and the canteen had discharged its wagonautic duty, Panier and Blanc vociferously called A. T. Ramp to read his sonnet for the day, which he did, as follows:

To Margaret, My Wife.

Come, love!—The sofa by the winter fire!—
And, leaning, cosy-like, let's write a sonnet.
Come nearer, I'll remove thy wraps and bonnet.
Sweetly in unison we'll strike the lyre.
Ah! bless the jealous clasp! the clinging knot!
I've touched her cheek! I feel her bosom throbbing!
I see her conscious blushes heart's blood robbing!
The song? Break not this charm of happy lot!
My love! sit here—we will not sonnets write.
Draw nigher, love!—here on my trembling knee,
Enfolded in my arms. We'll sonnets live.
I cannot write. Why all the poetry's quite
Gathered within the swelling heart of me;
And that to thee—but not in verse—I'll give.

Mr. Ramp said, when he had finished with great applause, that he regarded the sonnet to his wife as his best; but she, like a jealous woman, insisted that the first and second were by far the best, although she couldn't see, for her part, why a strange woman should inspire a man like his own wife.

It was then moved by Panier, and seconded by Brutus, that the daily sonnet be adjourned. Carried, Ramp in the negative.

As we sat offering burnt offerings of fragrant tobacco in old mellow pipes, Brutus inscribed upon a large white fungus a marvelously sweet poem to Emma Jean, whom he addressed under the guise of a glen rose. I am sorry that I neglected to take a copy of this remarkable ode. The following stanza is all I can recall:

> Ah, Emma Jean! Ah, Emma Jean!
>   Rose o' the mountain glen;
> Thy bonnie e'en, wi' dewy sheen,
>   Lovely 'yond mortal ken,
> Have pierced wi' Cupid's cruel dart,
>   My winsome Emma Jean,
> Profoundly within my throbbing heart,
>   Wounding deep and keen.

Even the lazy pipe and the indolent *siesta* will come to untimely end, and now we are off again, soon finding leveler road among the gnarled dwarf beeches, lifting us gradually into the gap on the Tennessee line. Thence we climb by devious ways up amongst the dark spruces and balsams which crown the bluff heights, where elevation gives them their proper arctic climate. At last we are on top spinning along a beautiful road, in sight of the Cloudland Hotel, which occupies an elevation of almost seven thousand feet and nearly the highest point of the Roan. Undergoing the usual critical inspection of new-comers at a summer resort, we rubbed off, poured out libations to snakes, enjoyed a square dinner, dismissed our driver and team, and tried to look as if we belonged at Cloudland. Ben parted from us with abundant regrets; said he'd been many a round with drummers and tourists, but the Wagonauts took the cake. He dwelt especially upon the Christian recognition by the Wagonauts of a profound fact in broad humanity: that a driver, although he cannot change his skin, and he may have brought it with him from the Niger, as black as the ace of spades, yet has soles to save from snakes as well as the rest. Ben said that, while of course he'd rather be on the inner paleface circle, yet as a matter of creature comforts, it was something to have been recognized when the flowing bowl was sparkling.

In thirty years the changes in the Roan are confined to its hotel, outhouses, roads, fences, and telephone wire. Otherwise it is as I saw it last thirty-one years ago, when it was a remote, untenanted wild, without cabin or hut; its acres of fertile soil bare of timber, except where balsams and spruces skirt the bluff edges, and chiefly covered with vast patches of rhododendrons, acres of heathers, and natural meadows of various wild grasses, with here and there a space of two or three acres naked of soil—in mountain speech, a "cowlick." Great masses of glacier-marked granites, covered with beautiful lichens, are scattered over the ground. Changeable every hour in its varying aspects of mist and cloud, this grand old mountain is like the ever changing ocean, also unchangeable and ever the same.

I looked for but was unable to recognize

the huge flat rock on the top of which I spent a dismal night on my last visit here thirty-one years ago. Reaching the summit at twilight, prepared only for wild turkey shooting next day, a heavy rain and thunder storm came up, drenching the whole face of the mountain. Masses of flame and zigzag darts of fire played along the ground, lighting up with weird glare the green grass, the frowning spruces and firs, and the rugged granite masses. It rained all night. Fire was out of the question. The side of the mountain was one sheet of water. I crawled up on a huge flat rock and tried to think I was enjoying myself. The thunder rolled and crashed and growled along the ground, making grand music for Titans to dance stately minuets to; and the vivid lightning flashes furnished torchlight to dance by.

It was upon that trip that I saw the curious reflection upon the mist which is called the "Brocken mountain spectre," from its occurrence upon the Hartz mountains of Germany. I was broiling sundry bits of fragrant bacon by a fire I had succeeded in kindling.

Hearing what I took to be the call of a turkey, I turned to get my gun, and staggered back, for a moment appalled by the giant figure that loomed up before me in the mist, making threatening gestures as I recoiled and lifted my hands in momentary terror. Then it stood still as I stood trembling, as if it had me securely in the grasp of some spell I could not break. Like all good boys, I'd been called a bad boy until I half believed it; and few boys of seventeen can see the devil without blinking. Although I knew that it was but the fog spectre of the Roan, it was as terrible to me for a moment as if it had been a real Titan. It is so weird and uncanny that none can see it for the first time without a sense of awe.

To one who loves nature in all its varying aspects, without caring for its scientific side, the Roan is a source of perpetual delight, with its starry nights, its varying cloud effects, its sweeping mists, its glorious views of mountain, plain, and field, its bosky forest recesses, and deep gorges, its crystal springs, its rugged cliffs, fringed with dark firs and festooned with wild vines, its vast bald mountain plain, its riches of plant life, ferns and flowers. To the scientist it is a very treasure house, said to be, in its flora, the richest in the world. The student of natural history finds less to interest him, but still something. Here the robin nests and the snowbird digs and plants his cosy home beneath the edge of some mossy cushion; here the raven is heard hoarsely croaking, not cawing, sailing like the turkey buzzard, not flapping like the crow. Raven and eagle build here their nests amongst inaccessible crags, where only spruce and fir find footing. Poisonous snakes are unknown, and a small harmless serpent is rare; and by a wise provision of nature, here, where venomous snakes are not found, the invigorating air makes snake medicine a superfluity.

If a reference to history may be allowed, it is said that here, upon the bald plains of the Roan's highest peak, the forces from Tennessee and Virginia met on their way to King's Mountain, and Rev. Samuel Doak, D.D., offered a fervent Scotch Presbyterian prayer for the success of the expedition; and Sevier, Evans, and Shelby went on in full faith to the destruction of British power in America.

I reserve a further account of the Roan and our departure for the next and last chapter.

CHAPTER VI.

The point of one white star is quivering still,
Deep in the orange light of widening noon;
Beyond the purple mountains, through a chasm
Of wind-divided mist, the darker lake
Reflects it. Now it wanes; now it gleams again,
As the waves fade and, as the burning threads
Of woven cloud unravel in the pale air,
'Tis lost and, through yon peaks of snow,
The roseate sunlight quivers. (Shelley.)

THE Roan is the true home of the clouds and rightly named Cloudland, as the centering point of all the fogs and mists of the valleys below, for leagues around, to which they gather and whence they disperse upon their fructifying and cooling missions to the lower mountains, valleys, and distant hills and plains. Notwithstanding a large condensation upon soil, rocks and vegetation, the air is pure, cool, and seldom unpleasantly moist.

The Roan is unsurpassed for the beauty

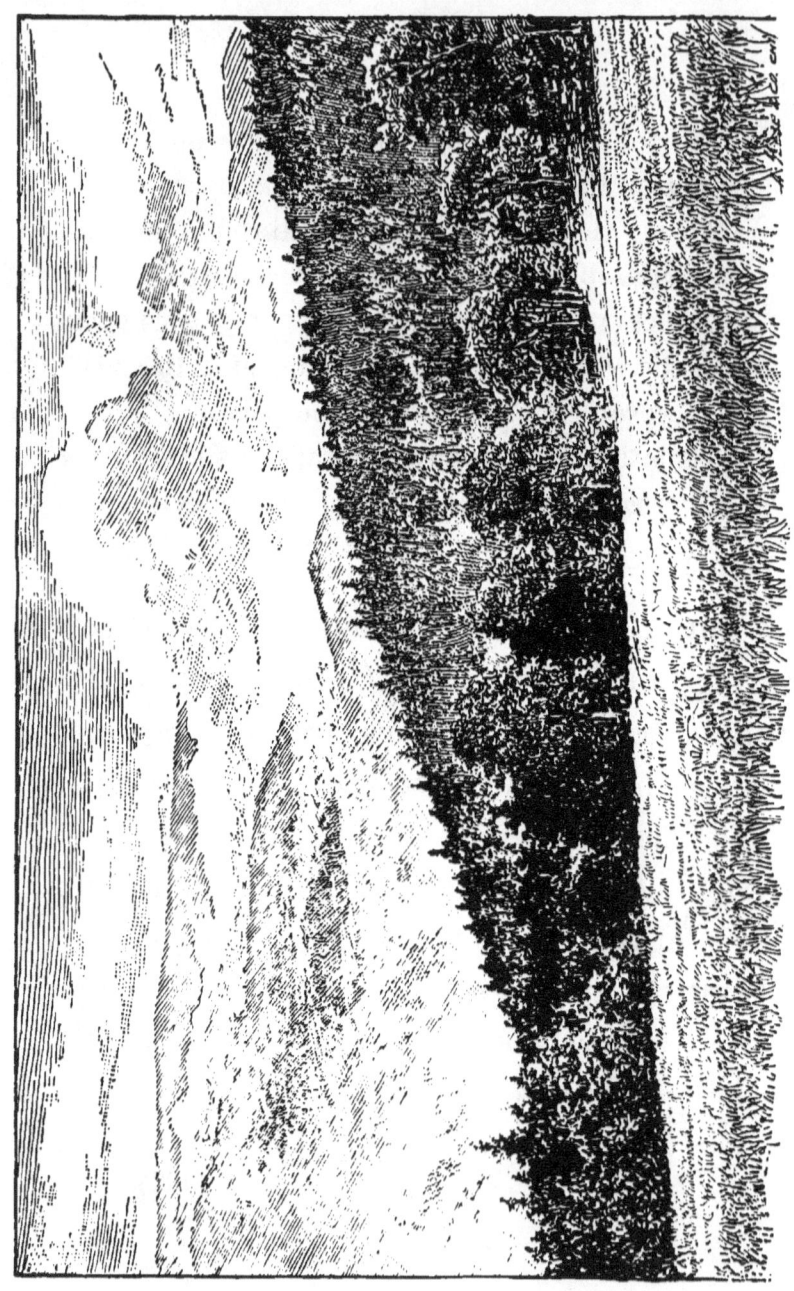

CLOUD EFFECTS.

of its cloud effects. In all that is grandest in nature it stands supreme: in a million changeful effects of mist in valleys and upon mountain sides below; in dark rain clouds in the lowlands and upper mountain slopes; in climbing clouds sweeping up the ridges, attracted by the cool mountain top; in far thunder and the sheen of broad flashing and sharp and zigzag darts of lightning; in clouds sweeping across the summit, veiling its distant peaks, creating weird and singular effects; in nigh rain storm, with thick darkness and thunder and lightning of rare sublimity and grandeur.

We stand upon Sunrise Rock astride the narrow cleft that marks the State line, and yonder to the east, a little by south, towers in gloomy grandeur the great cloud-compeller of all the mountain region of the Blue Ridge and the Alleghanies, the lofty fir-covered peaks of the grim Black, to whom even the Roan doffs his cloudy chapeau as the very Jove of cloud-compellers and storm-gatherers. Further eastward is Lynnville Gap, with the bold, square front of Table

Rock upon one side, and the Hawkbill upon the other; and the pale, far blue of the Blue Ridge, stretching in the dim distance, overlooking the Piedmont and tidewater regions to the east and coastward. To the south towers the cloud-capped summit of the Great Bald, himself no laggard in the business of cloud-gathering. Further westward are the Big Butt range and Rich Mountain group, and in the far distance, Paint Rock, near the Asheville road. Nearer, almost at our feet, the long, low Buffalo Ridge stretches unbroken for miles across the head of the great valley of East Tennessee, separating valley-plains from mountain regions and lying near Jonesboro. Beyond this and over its southern end the beautiful valley of the Nola Chuckee extends along the base of the mountains, westward to its junction with the valley of the French Broad, whence they go to form the Tennessee.

Further northward is the valley of East Tennessee, from the Alleghanies to the Cumberland Table Land, embracing the valley of the Nola Chuckee, of the further French

Broad, of Holston, Watauga, Clinch, and Powell Rivers and the peaks of Haystack, Chimney Top, and House Mountains. To the northwest the dim outline of the Cumberland Mountains looms up in the grey light. Further east and north lie far vague lines of mountain in West Virginia. Yonder north by east a river has cut an opposite ridge squarely down upon both sides for many miles, leaving a curious gap and scooping out a deep channel and a broad plain between the opposite sides. Northward lie the Virginia mountains, the tall Grandfather and the Peaks of Otter.

We have now boxed the compass, sweeping around the horizon with the far view, looking into North and South Carolina, Tennessee, Georgia, West Virginia, Kentucky, and Virginia. In the near lie the mountain regions of Tennessee and North Carolina, one tumbled, jumbled, confused mass of peaks and ranges, mountain piled upon mountain, as if the Titans had fought their last battle here and piled Ossa upon Pelion.

All around us, in the deep valleys, narrow

SUNSET ROCK.

gorges, high vales and broad valley-plain of the Toe—a vile corruption of a beautiful Indian name—about Bakersville and Burnsville, lies one calm, motionless, sleeping sea of white mist, pale and ghostly, with broad bays, deep inlets, and winding rivers. Every stream, where every valley has its winding brook, has furnished its share of white mist to fill up the valley. In this ocean of ghostly mist lie blue islands of mountain peaks, hilltops and ridges, bold, jutting headlands, with rocky front and long indented shore lines—cape, isthmus, promontory, and peninsula.

Over all this sea of white grimly stands the solemn Roan, its craggy ridges running, dark and rugged, down into the misty ocean like long, narrow capes. Presently will arise one mightier than the mountain ruler-by-night of the fogs and mists, and they will arise at the bidding of the glorious sun, and form a fleecy crown of glory about the lowering brow of old Roan.

The sun comes up unclouded. A flood of light bursts over hill and valley, mountain and plain. The blue western mountain sides sink deeper into the shadows; eastward all is aglow with rosy light; and now all the ocean of mist is astir, slowly lifting, breaking up into fragments, climbing rugged heights toward various condensing points, to drift gradually up to the summit of the Roan.

If one could grasp, much less describe, the myriad changing effects of light and shadow upon this fairy scene of enchantment: colors, hues, tints, shades, and names! With his boasted gift of speech man has named perhaps a hundred—not so many. Here every infinitesimal point in the broad landscape of thousands of square miles of mountain, hill, valley, and plain, with its generally prevailing hues of greens, blues, yellows, reds, and their infinite variety, has each its own peculiar hue. The same tint is one in one light, another in another light; one hue in the shade, varying in intensity with the varying shadows, until one is bewildered with the infinite variety of shade, tone, light, and color. Under the glorious sun's Prospero wand it is a very scene of enchantment.

The scene shifts. The transition has been so rapid that we are astonished when a swift-sailing wave of mist from the ocean below comes flying up, rounding the headland peak whereon we stand. In a moment we are in the midst of thick darkness, with naught visible, save the barren rock at our feet. Changes of mist and cloud, shadow and sunlight are made by the great scene-shifter with such surprising rapidity and startling effects that now the cloud by which we were enveiled has vanished. Far clouds, or rather mists —for clouds lie as high above the mountain top as they lie above the valleys below—are still climbing the ridges beneath us; the sky is almost clear, the long ridges and towering peaks of the Roan are again visible; clouds float lazily overhead, courting the genial sunlight. The curtain that shut out the light and the earth has faded like a dream.

There is something awe-inspiring in these thick clouds and rapid transitions. The tourist without a guide, or a thorough knowledge of woodcraft, must wait until he regains his senses, or he is likely to come out of such veil of mist with everything looking changed, weird, and uncanny and to lose his way. Many parties have thus been lost. A Supreme Judge of Tennessee came out of one of the Roan fogs unable to find a single precedent for his guidance, and had to be looked up by a lawyer like any ordinary litigant. A pair of lovers spent a night and two days wandering about the slopes of the Roan, and then failed to return thanks for being found. It has never been satisfactorily determined whether they were befogged before or during the mist-fall in which, presumably, they lost their way. Since they were wedded soon after, it made no great difference. The happy swain is said to have returned thanks to the fog-spectre of the Roan for a prompt consent, following a long waiting, which had promised to be longer.

Sometimes on a clear day, one may see a cloud gathered in the lowlands, whence one knows not. There is a brief lighting up of the gathered mass, with sharp lightning flashes, a distant rumbling of thunder, and the cloud grows darker, bright above and angry purple upon its shadowed edges. Rain descends and we may mark the dark, wet streak upon the ground as the cloud passes and fades away, leaving the rain area glistening and smiling in renewed sunlight.

Sometimes one may see a dozen local rains in a day or even a dozen local rains going on at once in the wide expanse of view from the Blue Ridge to the far distant Cumberland Mountains. It is surprising how small is the area of such rain, when to one enveloped in the cloud of such rain storm the whole heavens appear dark.

Now a thin mist veils one-half of Lion Bluff, so that its grim rocks and dark firs show weirdly in the sunlit mist, like some enchanting, dissolving view, while the other half stands the more darkly and boldly outlined in the full light. Lion Bluff is so called from a more than fancied resemblance to a lion couchant, as the law hath it, with body well defined and shaggy head clearly outlined in a bold headland of rugged rocks, flanked by a rocky ridge, covered with dark spruces.

Here is also to be seen a piece of natural statuary grander than any artist ever cut from marble. A bold granite feminine head, with Egyptian headdress and cast of feature, projects from the side of a great bluff, with low, massive forehead, well defined, expressive nose, heavy brow, well curving lips—a figure as grand and gloomy as the Sphinx and somewhat resembling it in outline. It is a strong, solemn, reflective face, with vast eyes fixed on futurity in deep, solemn repose, as if meditating upon profound questions, involving the beginning and the end, the woes and the sorrows of Titans. No fancy is needed to make out the features, and the profile grows sharper and clearer the nigher one approaches and with each successive visit.

Alas! if one had the brilliant descriptive powers of a Ruskin, with his wordy and glittering wealth of adjective and mixed metaphor, jumbled like mixed pickles in a bottle and as cold, lifeless, icy, and often as beautiful as a polar iceberg, with George Eliot's divine power of giving life and breath, thought and motion and moral qualities to whatever she touches, one might describe the Roan.

The Wagonauts grew restless. The Roan is snakeless as Iceland. The demijohn of snake medicine fell to zero. As the Jason of the expedition, I suggested that we keep the holy Sabbath by a solemn walk down to Roan Station. If I said six miles, I didn't mean to mislead. Brutus is sternly opposed to walking. He is so opposed to leg action that I would expect difficulty in securing his acceptance of a legacy. It was necessary to convince him that Roan Station was only six miles distant, of which three could be cut off by bridle paths. I cannot tell a lie, and Panier undertook to convince him. At 10 o'clock of a peaceful Sunday, we bade goodbye to Cloudland, up anchor for home, down the steep descent, taking the by-paths through the moist recesses of the thick forests which clothe mountain sides, that are destined at no distant day to be covered with smiling meadows and fields and flock-bearing pasture lands, to the very summit. With all day before us and the last quart that could be squeezed out of the demijohn, we ran on slow schedule, making frequent halts at cool gushing springs in fairy haunts and sylvan glens, where deep shadows and moss-grown rocks invited to repose.

Getting involved in a tripartite discussion of the universal order and the "eternal fitness of things," the usual thing happened. We forgot the particular and lost our run of the concrete in our absorption in the general and the abstract, and lost our way. Observation of ridges and valleys and Jason's knowledge of woodcraft soon set us right. With an adjournment, *sine die*, of all questions concerning the general order of the universe, we reached the great tramway and our road six miles above Roan Station.

At the first house, except a small cabin, high up the mountain side, I proposed buttermilk. An affected fear of dogs, but a real desire to put the best foot foremost, led Brutus and Panier to elect me to explore. To my astonishment a well-dressed, elegant, and handsome young woman came to the door and gave me permission to call in my friends.

I had seen a little girl swinging, most unmountainlike, in a hammock in the back porch; but I had supposed that she was some tourist's child. Soon a foaming pitcher of fresh buttermilk, a roll of yellow butter, and (here in the mountains) a loaf of Graham bread lay upon the table before us. "Isn't there something before eating?" asked Brutus who seldom neglects anything. "Grace?" I asked, innocently. "Well yes—something of that kind—libations—drink offerings to the ophidian powers for safety from snakes," returned Brutus. "Ah, yes, I'd forgot," I replied, and, turning to the young lady, said: "My friends like sugar in their buttermilk." I will take my book oath that she came back with real cube sugar, three glasses and spoons and a jug—that's English, you know—of cold water. "They never drink water in their buttermilk," I said, when she'd safely deposited the ingredients. "No, but you'll need it," she answered, and discreetly retired, while I pulled out the last of the demijohn and brewed three toddies that Jove might have sipped with the ambrosia at an Olympian banquet; and then we proceeded to precipitate ourselves violently on the outside of three gallons of buttermilk and a whole loaf of Graham bread.

When our luncheon came to an end, the young lady came to invite us to rest upon the shady back porch. Brutus and Panier, who never recognize a good thing when they see it, began to say that we must move on to Roan Station. I thanked her and asked her to sit with us and tell us something of the mountains. We were joined by her mother, a refined, well-preserved woman of no extravagant number of years. The mother, two daughters, and a little girl lived here alone, coming from Bakersville, N. C. They saw little company except tourists, and were clearly cultivated, educated people, and one of the daughters, we learned was a contributor to some Eastern magazine.

I soon observed Brutus growing restless under my allusion to his wife. I knew that his impressible heart was off again. I knew that he would find some indirect way to assault me and tax the Jason of the Wagonautic expedition with unkindness in alluding to his wife, without mentioning the exact ground of his anger.

We'd scarcely got behind the laurel that lined the broken tramway when he burst out with: "I've been lied to—egregiously lied to."

"I suppose you want me to lie about your wife."

"I was speaking of the lie about that six miles, when it's twelve to Roan Station. As for that stale joke about a wife, I've had enough of that, too." I offered to go back and swear that Brutus walks in maiden meditation, fancy free.

When we'd made a half mile, Brutus turned and gazed at the cosy cabin, called for the canteen, sat down upon a log, and wrote and read as he wrote, bringing forth the following tribute to his latest flame and a sad farewell to Emma Jean:

Ode to Truth.

The canteen? yes; the cup too, please!
(O keg!)
Yes, truth you side the Pyrenees—
(Canteen!)

THE WAGONAUTS ABROAD. 125

Ye gods! look there! the pair o' knees
I've got wi' sliding, scrambling;
O'er granite rocks! this mountain rambling!
   (O keg!)
O had we Alcibiades!*
And his little team of atomies!
   (Canteen!)
This walking's not a Christian grace!—
   (O keg!)
It's only fit for grovelling race,
   (Canteen!)
As for this rambling, metamorphic!
   (O keg!)
I'll try and be as philosophic
'S I can. You say it's pleasure, fun!—
   (O keg!)
I'll sum it up, when the journey's done—
"Summit up!"—"Always some 'at up?"—
   (O keg!)
Come, Panier, I would rather sup,
Short-spooned, wi' the devil, than that punster
Should play 'pun me what you call fun, sir—
   (Canteen!)
Where was I? On the Pyrenees!
   (O keg!)
And then these trousers—pair o' knees,
Abraded, torn, unpatched, contused,

---

*One of the many names given our driver.

Somehow got my wits confused—
Some sort of tangled brain disease-
    (Canteen!)
Aye, truth yon side the Pyrenees
Is error on the other side—
So thin lines true from false divide!
    (O keg!)
I think 'twas said by Gallic Paschal,
Or other mediæval rascal.
    (O keg!)
I'll prove, in metres amphibrachian,
It's just as true o' th' Appalachian
System, they call the Alleghany—
As lovely mountain range as any
  Boasting Gaul or Swiss can brag on—
Mountain that we've driv'n our drag on.
    (O keg!)
On t'other side the Unicoi,
I roved a lithesome-hearted boy,
    (O keg!)
Till, meeting bonnie Emma Jean,
    (Canteen!)
I melted 'neath her love-lit e'en,
    (Canteen!)
If ever love in heart was true,
    (O keg!)
True love did my soft heart imbue,
    (Canteen!)

My soul was fierce aflame wi' true-love—
As true as ever rhymed wi' coo-dove—
As true as ever from above,
The constant heart of man did move.
      (O keg!)
And yet I'd scarce the mountain crossed,
      (Canteen!)
My soul wi' passion wildly tossed,
When yon sweet maid in yonder cabin—
Cosy enow to lodge Queen Mab in—
A-nesting sweetly in ivy bowers,
Where purple-clustered laurel flowers,
Lean down to kiss the murm'ring waves,
Of brook that o'er rough ledges raves,
Resounding hollow through cool cave,
Where lowly summer blossoms lave
Their petals in the crystal brook,
And coy trout woo the angler's hook—
      (O keg!)
Bless me! again I'm sadly lost,
      (Canteen!)
'Pon brooklet wavelet tempest tossed—
      (O keg!)
Ah yes! I'd just the mountain crossed—
Dividing line twixt false and true—
Twixt cloud-false skies and love's true-blue—
      (Canteen!)
When truth I found to error turned—
The love that in my heart had burned,
      (O keg!)

Was false, a lie, a mere delusion,
A jumbled, hazy, wild confusion,
A self-deceit, a mere dissembling,
As I stood by yon maiden, trembling
With true-love, this side Unicoi,
A love-lorn man, no longer boy.
   (O keg!)
O, then, I saw the truth with ease,
That truth yon side the Pyrenees—
   (O keg!)
(Yes, Panier! thanks! a bit o' cheese—
   (O keg!)
And let me have the corkscrew, please)—
   (Canteen!)
To error rank had been transmuted,—
A truth that can't now be disputed!—
And universal is the law:
It's just as true o' th' Unicoi—
As gospel-true o' th' Appalachian—
   (Canteen!)
(These rhymes will split thy tubes eustachian?)
And just as true o' th' Alleghany,
Kaatskills, Sierras, Youghiogheny.
   (O keg!)
We change the sky and keep the mind,
But leave what's in the soul behind.
   (Canteen!)
Farewell, my winsome Emma Jean,
   (Canteen!)

Farewell, fore'er, thy love-lit e'en,
        (Canteen!)
Ah, maiden o' the log-locked cabin!—
Just big enough to hide Queen Mab in!—
I'm now, forever, only thine!
Be thou, O be, forever mine.
        (O keg!)   (R. L. Brutus.)

Then the solemn *cortége* sadly moved on, and slowly wound its devious way down the valley, leading Brutus, and guiding his halting steps, as he continually turned to gaze backward towards his true-love this side the Unicoi. "Six miles yet," sighed Brutus, "and not a drop left."

Our way now lay through a wild, broken country by the side of a clear winding stream. Sometimes we traveled the road, but oftener the broken tramway. At one point, where we were on the opposite side from the road, with a dense laurel screen shutting out the view, we prepared for a cool plunge into an icy stream. How were we to know that a neighborhood path ran just inside the fence? How were we to know or conceive that rustic swains and maidens were going to desecrate the holy Sabbath by coming along that path upon a Sunday berrying expedition? While sitting on the fence beneath the shade of a wide-spreading birch, waiting to cool off, a covey of dreadful sunbonnets loomed up in full view. "Hold on there, girls," I shouted, plunging into the pool head-foremost, like a muskrat. Two jolly urchins came up, holding their sides with laughter, and I told them to tell the party that we would seek modest hiding whilst they went by. "We hain't a carin'," said one of the boys. "I know you don't care, you little imp, but we do," I said, "and the girls do." Just then a young mountaineer came by, and we came to terms. The tittering procession went solemnly by, with sunbonnets all set indiscreetly sidewise, and they had scarcely got by when Brutus launched himself into the pool like a bull frog, exclaiming as he went: "D—— 'f I can stand those thorns any longer."

As we walked lazily down the last mile, Panier thought it best to cross the creek to the road. Poising himself with his umbrella under his arm, upon the smooth top of a great "biscuit rock," he leaped for the top of another. His foot slipped, and he sat down in the water, with the huge white rock between his legs and the umbrella under his arm and back contemptuously upstream. "Why don't you hoist your umbrella," cried Brutus, as we rolled convulsed upon the ground.

Next morning our party of Wagonauts came down for a plunge in the creek before a delicious breakfast at Roan Station hotel. While we were out enjoying the clear waters of Doe River, a waiter came to the proprietor with: "Boss, dem gemmen whar come in las' night done skip de house."

"Why, George," said the proprietor; "they looked like gentlemen."

"Cyarnt allus tell, boss; I knowed dey wuz sompin wrong ez soon as I ketched de eye o' dat'n wid de black mustacher an' looked at de cut o' dat little un wid de light hyar an' mustacher. I lay dey done overpuswaded dat big fat man dey called Mr. Ramp. He looked like a plum gemman."

"They didn't take their baggage, did they, George?"

"Dat dey didn't; dat bargage hain't got nuffin in't nohow 'cept three empty quart bottles; I seed em a strainin' dem larst night."

A rail journey of two hours through the canyon of the Doe, as wild and as rugged as any on the Rocky Mountains, brought us to Johnson City and the end of the first wagonautic expedition.

NOTE.—The suspicion that our party had skipped the house is literally true, except that Brutus was the excepted party and described as a "plum gemman."

PART SECOND.
IN THE MOUNTAIN WILDS OF SOUTHWESTERN NORTH CAROLINA.

DRAMATIS PERSONÆ.

H. M. Doak, Clerk U. S. Circuit Court - *A. T. Ramp.*
G. II. Baskette, Editor *Nashville Banner* - *Gid II. Panier.*
Dr. R. L. C. White, K. G. S., K. P. - *Dr. R. Elsie Blanc.*

QUALLA CHEROKEE SCHOOL

THE WAGONAUTS ABROAD.

CHAPTER I.

Infandum regina, Jubes renovare dolorem.

KNOXVILLE, 12 M. Three Wagonauts, escaped from the dog-days' heat of Nashville, dash gaily down Gay, the main street of picturesque Knoxville, toward the long bridge across the Holston. What changes! In these streets I have seen—and borne my humble part—revolution and counter-revolution; witnessed here riot, there murder. Yonder I saw the Union desperado, Douglas, wounded by the Confederate desperado, Wash Morgan, and a few days after I saw Douglas shot—assassinated—by a shot from the Lamar House windows. I have drilled squads, companies, and battalions along these streets and over yonder hills and hep-hepped over all these hereabouts. On this Gay Street, in 1865, myself disguised in the latest

New York fashion, and just from Appomattox, I saw seven or more returned Confederates brutally knocked down and beaten by Federal soldiers. I spent the afternoon in pious retirement and took the earliest train for change of air and scene. Knoxville has changed and yet it retains its individuality, social worth, and the ancient stamp of its founders.

On receipt of information concerning the abundance and venomous character of copperheads in the portion of North Carolina we were about to visit, the Wagonauts provided two kegs of antidote and a canteen as provision against such breakage as left us exposed to rattlesnakes in our last journey.

As we bowl along Gay Street our company consists of R. Elsie Blanc, ruddy blonde, auricomous, fourteen stone weight; G. H. Panier, blonde, shadlike—late shad—angular, nine stone; and A. T. Ramp. Our driver is a decided brunette, rejoicing in the Italian name of Lorenzo, known to us, in rainy seasons as Jupiter Pluvius, in drought as Pomery Sec. As to our team, both bays, but

Frank alone entitled to the bay, Jim's chief use was to fill a place at the off-wheel as a sort of balance wheel. Panier lugubriously remarked, as we hung up on the side of a mountain, that the only mistake made was in failing to provide a seat in the wagon for Jim.

Business men display varying tastes in their summer diversions. One seeks to change the sky without losing the comforts and luxuries of civilization. For him there are no delightful sharp contrasts, no delicious lights and shades, no sweet, enjoyable alternations of the rough and smooth of life; and he wants none of these. Our theory of diversion is complete change from all the conditions of daily life. Hence we sought for this summer the wild solitudes of the remote and almost inaccessible mountains of south-western North Carolina. To endure the storm, to let the rain pour on, to climb alpine heights, to thread tangled laurel thickets, to wade cool mountain streams and cast the hungry trout line, to sleep on the ground, in deserted cabins, in wayside churches and schoolhouses, to say to the elements, "blow ye winds and crack your cheeks; we tax not ye elements with unkindness; pour on, we can endure;" to relish rough fare with ostrich appetites, was our aim in going to this region, where the aboriginal Cherokee is yet found upon his autochthonal ground and where are found the highest peaks this side of the Sierras.

The outfit of such party is a matter of commissary and quartermaster wisdom. We had a strong carriage, with three seats, capable of being completely closed up, a pair of horses, bucket, axe, hatchet, monkeywrench, and extra horseshoes. Our edibles consisted of canned corned beef, canvased beef, and breakfast bacon, a baked ham, butter, biscuits, sardines, caviare, coffee, lemons, olives, with ample cooking utensils, table ware, pipes and smoking tobacco. No cigars. Two mysterious kegs containing something ruddy and sunlit, which seemed greatly to comfort Panier and Blanc, continually replenished a half-gallon canteen. I have never been able to ascertain what those kegs contained, but I think it was about three gallons apiece. A double blanket each and a rubber blanket completed our outfit. Thus provided, we made two hundred and fifty miles with comparative comfort and delicious hardships.

Our way led us over the road by which Nola Chuckee Jack (John Sevier) was wont to lead his backwoods knights to the defense of the young settlement of what is now Sevier County, to launch them like a thunderbolt upon the Erati Cherokees. As we drew near to Sevierville, the foothills of the tall Alleghanies lifted their low, steep barriers, vine-covered, "rock-ribbed and ancient as the sun." To the right and left and before us opened the broad valley of the two Pigeons, Big and Little, and their branches and tributaries. Night drew on, with songs of cicada, whippoorwill, toad, tree-frog and bull-frog, the gleam of firefly, and meteor flash of lightning bugs in meadow and field, and along alder-fringed and willow-lined streams, and in dark valleys. The gloomy way is enlivened with song and jest. Panier and Blanc talk far better than they sing. For diversion I was forced to sing myself; but then I can sing—a fact that even Jim recognized. This exasperating animal lay down in a swamp and signified his unwillingness to endure further toil for any prospect of oats, wild or tame. Panier and Blanc exhibited their mean envy by remarking that such singing would unhorse any animal. I alighted and walked, singing a caviare from Trovatore. Panier says it's *cavatina*; but Panier is a purist; for 'twas "caviare to the general." Jim arose from his muddy couch and followed me, entranced, as the wild beasts followed Orpheus. Great is the power of music.

At last Jim consented to reach the ford at Sevierville. Here was a go. Neither our Ferguson, nor any one of us, knew the ford. We assailed a neighbor house with shrill "house-ahoy!" without avail. Assuming the superior knowledge of a man who's once been there, I took the reins and plunged in boldly, no matter how coldly the rough river ran. Fording a mountain river, with its swift currents, rough rapids, and deep holes, and the night as dark as Erebus, is no child's play. When we reached the further bank, I found Blanc and Panier each seated astride a keg. We reached Sevierville at 10 o'clock, finding the tavern chock-a-block with Methodist preachers attending Conference. Blanc and I, in reply to the white-stoled landlady, declared we could put up with lodgings and sup at breakfast. Panier's insatiable maw arose in instant rebellion and asked for pie —said he could manage to wear out the night with pie. That man will eat anything. It was well that Panier prevailed and we had supper; for we lost that night, wrestling with the voracious cimex lectularius, armed and with lance in rest, by actual weight, two pounds of good red blood apiece.

Pale, worn, and weary, we staggered in to breakfast, where we found that uncounted flocks of chickens had assembled on the table, anxious to be eaten by the Methodist Conference. Our Methodist brethren looked with pious suspicion upon our canteen and kegs; but we disarmed suspicion by explaining that we were going as palefaced missionaries to the Cherokee Reservation.

Leaving Sevierville and taking our way up the north fork of Little Pigeon, our road led us diagonally across the spurs, ridges, and foothills of the Alleghanies. The streams now began to change from the dirty, milky blue of limestone regions into the clear brown of sandstone hills and then into the bright yellow, clear, sunny waters of the matamorphic rock country. As we climb up and up, bright waters flash forth from deep coverts, and brooks babble sweetly and noisily down from gloomy heights above; ever more and more embowered in thick-set laurel and ivy, which here replace the willows and alders of the lower lands. Crossing ridges, climbing hills, going straight up gorges and valleys, we enter Cocke County, aiming across foot ridges, to reach our only practical route by Mt. Sterling Gap, or "Starling," as they call it here. Crossing thus, from the waters of the Little Pigeon to the beautiful valley of the Cosby, cheered by Panier's recitation of a beautiful original poem, which nothing but his modesty has kept out of print, we begin to beseech the obdurate natives for corn.

The story of our further wanderings is reserved for the next chapter, wherein is also something of our camp and of the natives and what they thought of the kegs.

CHAPTER II.

We are such stuff as dreams are made of,
And our little lives are rounded with a sleep.

AS we drove down to Cosby Creek an inviting house chilled our ardor for outdoors. Dusk was drawing on and a ravishing odor of frying ham filled the valley. A native was chopping wood at a wood pile.

"Stranger, is this Cosby?"

"I reckon hit ar," replied the woodchopper, cutting us off with a surly tone, without looking up or knocking off work. Surliness to strangers is something unusual in the mountains.

"Any corn in this neighborhood?"

"Dunno; corn's powerful scyace."

"Could we stay all night?"

"Dunno; you-uns mout go up the creek an' see."

"Drive on," said Blanc; "you axed him a

civil question and he gave you a sharp answer and went on axing the wood pile."

"His axions spoke louder than his words," said Panier. This sort of execrable punning is what I have to endure. I never wittingly indulge in that sort of wit.

Crossing Cosby, we drove up a large clear stream, winding along the center of a fertile, well-cultivated valley. No corn was to be had at any of the many houses along the way. At a country store a number of natives gave us good advice. We could camp at a church a mile up the river. Corn could be had, always three or four miles off the road. At last a "mountain boomer," who lived nigh where we expected to camp, would sell us oats, but no corn. When the case of Jim and Frank seemed desperate, a man who'd just bought a half bushel of shelled corn consented to exchange it for forty cents' worth of the contents of the keg—a transaction in which the United States had an interest, which it has lost by the running of the statute of limitations.

In a few minutes we had a rousing fire

crackling and lighting up a grove of fine hemlocks, which surrounded the church; and Ceres was sent to buy oats.

"No wonder dat man hain't gwyne to sell no corn; he's got eight chillin, an he gwyne to need dat corn." This is a prolific region.

The unfortunate man was about thirty. Early marriages, wholesome air and water, a reckless disregard for consequences, and ignorance of Malthus make from eight to a dozen children the rule of households hereabout. Panier enviously remarked that they seemed to raise 'em by coveys. Thus it comes about that these mountain regions have furnished more people to the great West than any other hive of human beings, New England not excepted.

A combined church and schoolhouse occupies the centre of a grassy grove on the banks of the Cosby. The stars are out; the katydids fill woodlands and mountain sides with sweet music; toad-frog and tree-frog make the valley vocal with wild melody, and all of nature's night voices make a sublime Wagnerian symphony. The smoke of our camp fire spreads itself amongst dark spruce boughs in spectre forms; the bright fire lights up black pine branches, casts weird shadows upon dark masses of foliage and flares with flickering light down long ghostly vistas, deep into the thick wood, lighting up dark trunks, down the long corridors of our sylvan halls. The neighbor creek bubbles and roars a few yards away as it bounds along upon its long journey from the crests of the Alleghanies to the Gulf of Mexico.

The steaming pot is bubbling and singing gleefully, purring with self-satisfaction as it brews that genuine gift of the gods, black coffee, which, by and by, Panier and Blanc will spoil with sugar and add insult to spoliation by lacing it with good liquor, thus spoiling two good things. Broad slices of canvased beef broil and sputter on the coals. Three forked spits, cut from neighbor boughs, hold slices of fragrant breakfast bacon— "streak and streak"—to the fire, browning and broiling, dripping upon toasted bread. By and by will be spread here a feast for the gods. Already such sweet incense ascends amongst spruce and pine boughs and up into the empyrean, with such savors of steaming coffee, toasting bread, and broiling meats, that old Jove on high Olympus disdains his lean fare of nectar and ambrosia, and enviously begins to thunder in the west.

"The canteen?" "Ah, Panier, it was you who first thought of the canteen at lunch," said Blanc. A light nip fresh from that mysterious keg would not harm an infant before supper. Blanc has had the canteen cooling in the creek, not unmindful himself of grog hour. Two to one; well I don't wish to be drenched, and I accept the inevitable. "Hold on there, 'Pete,'" cried Blanc as I made a close inspection of "Job's Coffin" over the fat, laughing side of the smiling canteen.

Now comes the coffee-cooling process. There's nothing so hot as a tin cup; but there's an appetizing delay and a lingering delight in pitching the dark cherry fluid from one tin cup to another after the fashion of Canova's Hebe, as she is represented pitching the matutinal cocktail for the gods on Olympus. We linger lovingly about the outspread feast, as the gods at Troy snuffed with delight the sweet savors of acceptable sacrifice. And now we fall to—

> Then, horn for horn, we stretch an' stryve;
> Deil tak the hin'most on we drive;
> Till a' our weel-swalled kytes, belyve,
>   Are stretched like drums.

The meal over, old man Panier "bethankit hums" and pipes are filled and we "lie like gods reclined, careless of mankind," stretched upon our blankets before the fire, with knapsacks for pillows, dreamily gazing up into the spruce boughs, upon the flickering lights and dancing shadows and through narrow openings into the starry heavens and up to where the peaks of the Great Smoky stand grim, dark and silent, guarded by a serried line of firs and spruces, faintly lit by the white beams of the setting moon; and "the place became religion."

Anecdote, retort and jest go round, as pipes are refilled and the canteen goes round. Would that I could Boswell Panier's and Blanc's ready wit, infinite humor, and light philosopy, so genial, bright, and sparkling, when first uncorked; so malapropos and cold, when gathered and recorded, like all gathered and recorded wit, whether of Sydney Smith, Douglas Jerrold, or Hood, ceasing to be wit when coldly printed without its circumstance and occasion.

Conversation now took a melancholy turn and dropped into a sentimental vein. It is the camp. All three had served the Confederacy from " Eend to eend." It is the camp —a perfect reproduction of the old days. We can imagine camp fires to the right, camp fires to the left, camp fires in front and rear —stacked arms, furled banners, tired men, flitting about the blazing fires, preparing the soldier's frugal meal, playing cards, smoking, reclining, dreaming of home, laughing, jesting, singing. Back again come crowding upon the memory high hopes, divine love for a nation newborn, wild, enthusiastic affection for a young banner that went down never dishonored. As we dreamed and talked in broken sentences, what if a silent tear bedewed the ground? God help the poor spirit upon either side of our great and both-sides-honoring struggle who can ever forget the sentiments proper to his own side and part! He is no true American, be he South or North man.

Alas! it fades; it is not real; but a faint simulacrum. The magician, memory, has called up an Alhambra view of a Boabdil court, a scene of enchantment, a mere mockery, to taunt the steadfast soul and its sweet memories of hopes, fears, and comradeship.

Our man of the oats and of corn unsparable and the quiver full of little arrows, came over to pay us a visit—a genuine mountain boomer—a name taken from a little black mountain squirrel, which I have not heard of lately. Our visitor has never been ten miles away from his own spring branch. He is overwhelmed with awe at the sight of Panier's breech-loading shotgun. His father was a Federal soldier; but no armed force ever entered this quiet valley. His mouth and eyes opened wide when Panier told him that we came from Nashville, three hundred miles away. I expected him to exclaim, as the old lady did when Daniel Webster told her he was from Boston, one hundred miles distant: "Law! stranger, how kin you live so fur off?" The canteen was passed and barely touched. "Drink hearty, stranger, we've plenty."

"No, I'm bleeged," said he, "I hain't had a drink fur nigh on to two year. I jest drink fur neighborness. I'm a settin' up late; but I'd lose a night jest to hyar you-uns talk."

One of the Wagonauts grew poetical and recited an ode to night. Observing the effect upon our visitor, he ventured into tragedy in wild, ranting style. It was better than any play to see the "boomer," with his head leaned back against the trunk of a tree, his eyes bleared wide, his mouth stretched from ear to ear, and his hands clasped in mute admiration. When the farewell of Othello to war came to an end, he drew a long breath, and after a moment's silence exclaimed, "You-uns kin speak, shore; I hain't never hyerd nothin' like that;" and he hadn't.

Our visitor departed; sleep began to close tired eyelids and the mind began to wander off among the lights and shadows, to climb ascending smoke wreaths, to nod with spectral shadows and weird forms under the overarching spruce boughs and to replace the waking realities with the unreal of half asleep.

Sonorus began to snore in the wagon; and the fire burned low. Signs of all Jove to come rushing down before morning warned us to make down our beds of fragrant spruce boughs and fern within the church. Stretched luxuriously upon this sweetest smelling and most sleep-provoking of couches, I soon heard Panier wrestling in his dreams with vagrant "chiggers" caught on the mountain sides, and Blanc's snore musically "dirl roof and rafter," like the devil's fiddling in "Tam O'Shanter." I lay awake and gazed out at the majestical roof of boughs, swaying in the rising breeze, at the fading stars and gathering clouds and listened to the deep roar of the mountain stream, the sweet voices of insects, the shrill pantherlike cry of the nighthawk, the plaintive note of the whippoorwill, the low, solemn, melancholy soughing of the wind as it went sighing and wailing through the pines, like a lost spirit, until I fell into unbroken, dreamless sleep.

At dawn we shook off downy sleep and after this poetical operation, prosily called Aurora to turn out, feed his team, and make ready for the road. A plunge into a clear, cold pool and a moment's lying in the foaming waves of a boiling cascade dissipated all lingering drowsiness and stiffness from unwonted exercise, and whetted appetites to a fine edge. Breakfast was soon smoking, and I must here say that there's magic in Panier's touch of the coffee pot. The brown berry of the gods parts with its subtlest aromas under his deft touch. I am sorry to qualify this statement by a story of mutiny. As Jason of the Wagonauts and flag officer of this squadron I have established six bells—11 o'clock—as early enough for any Christian's grog—and the grog hour the world over. Panier came up with a cup containing sugar and water, and boldly demanded the canteen, making pretense of neuralgia and of really needing a drop. I sternly told him that if he was ill the surgeon of the expedition would settle with him out of the medicine chest, with his choice of a purge, an emetic, or a blister; but no grog upon any hypocritical pretence. I ought to say that I have been compelled to withdraw custody of the kegs from the surgeon and entrust them only to myself. Blanc here interposed with a bald statement about a touch of rheumatism, ridiculously limping up with a cup containing sugar, very little water and a sprig of what he called mint. "Not a drop," I said, "not a drop until six bells. Besides, if my botany's not at fault, that's not mint, but a plant of the solanum family, and possibly deadly poison." Blanc's narrow escape cast a gloom over the crew, and I was able to quell this rising mutiny. My botanical knowledge, which has been the subject of scurvy jests with Panier and Blanc, is now upon a better footing; so that I have been able, with fair credence, to call unknown plants by any big name that came handy.

As we were about starting, and Orestes had already assumed the reins, our visiting native came over to see us off. Declining grog and breakfast, he said he'd only come to "howdy, ez he'd never seed sich gentlemen afore."

"How far to Hopkins, on Big Creek?" was asked him.

"I jist dunno," he replied. "I jist dunno" seems to be a universal expression of blank ignorance about here.

Our direct route to the Cherokee country would have been by Catlettsburg, but that is impassable. It is our aim to-day to reach the foot of Big Smoky, across the ridges and spurs, which stretch northwardly from the main range. Vegetation has already perceptibly changed its character. Some plants have dropped out altogether, as we have gradually left the flora of the valleys for the plant life of the highlands. Late as it is, the chestnut trees are laden with white feathery blossoms, long ago shed in the valleys below us. Strange mutations! Blanc and Panier are just now in full autumnal chestnut fruitage, and I'm the victim of their spiny burrs and bitter nuts. The glades and hillsides are covered with tulip trees, which we miscall poplar, rarely the cottonwood, which is a true poplar, but seldom seen at this height, the red birch, the graceful pale-trunked white birch, linns, ash, wild cherry, cucumber magnolias, whose red fruit is said to be a substitute for rennet in cheese-making. Familiar lowland growths are sometimes represented by similar but unfamiliar varieties. The familiar bull-nettle grows with a longer stem, and a white flower has taken the place of our blue blossom. Along with our modest flowering nightshade is seen the bell-shaped flower of the deadly nightshade, the belladonna plant of the atropia family. The large palmetto fern of lower levels is mingled with many beautiful varieties, suited to this latitude or altitude, which is the same thing. The deadly crow plant grows here and there, a grasslike tuft. The fatal hemlock—locally so-called, although it is neither conia nor cicuta—with its luxuriant vinelike growth, mats every moist valley, dell, and glade. The conium, called in English hemlock, is supposed to be the plant which introduced Socrates to his dæmons in the realms of Pluto. The lowly mountain tea, with its birchlike flavor, grows upon every hillside. The bearberry, with a lovely flower resembling the Cherokee rose or the eglantine, grows with tropical luxuriance in low places, bearing a berry very like the Antwerp raspberry, its fruit a pleasant acid, its semi-vine stalk, hairy, low, and many branched, its leaf broad and grape-leaflike—a plant that should be cultivated for its flower if not for its fruit.

Before reaching the State line, which is erroniously located on the maps, we came to a mill and toll-gate upon an imaginary turnpike. I hope the meal of the old Giant Despair who keeps it justifies toll-taking— his turnpike doesn't. We declined to pay toll upon a "no thoroughfare;" and the sight of Panier's breach-loader induced him to offer us free transportation.

Panier and I, assisted by Demagogus and the whip, had great difficulty in keeping Blanc from making a speech at the State line. The Governor of North Carolina was here referred to and, in some way, the Governor of South Carolina was lugged in—how I never could tell. I think that Panier said it was a long time between Governors. To save time Blanc and I agreed to this absurd proposition, which leads me to reserve a further account of our journeyings and of the maiden of Big Creek until my next chapter.

CHAPTER III.

> Jura from her misty shroud,
> Answers joyous Alps that call to her aloud.
>
> (Byron.)

IN the last chapter I left Panier, Blanc, and myself at the State line, involved in some enigmatical matter concerning the Governors of North and South Carolina. Through the friendly mediation of Bacchus, who dropped the reins and passed the canteen, this was satisfactorily settled.

We have now passed over the interesting geological series between Knoxville and the Great Smoky—over limestone, shale, slate, micaceous slates—over "grey knobs" and "red knobs"—not at all attractively "knobby" to tourists with a balky horse. We've passed through, not over, the Chilhowie range, leaving the two ends of its sandstone ridges to the right and left of us as we approached Sevierville. We're now on what Dr. Safford, the State Geologist of Tennessee, calls the

Ocoee series, composed of conglomerates, sandstones, slates, and shales bordering on the metamorphic rocks.

Tennessee, it may be remarked in passing, while now a niggard in scientific research, owes its present rapid growth in wealth to the scientific forethought of its earlier men. In Dr. Troost, a naturalist, botanist, and natural historian of world-wide fame, and in his worthy successor, Dr. Safford, it stands foremost for the value, rather more than the amount of scientific work. As a result, when knowledge of its resources was most needed, just after the war between the States, the records made by Troost and Safford laid the State bare to the bottom. Would-be investors could see to the center of the earth, from the crests of the Alleghanies to the Mississippi— flora, fauna, and mineral wealth. Full of just pride to take scientific rank, our ancestors meant science; the result has been wealth; and yet the poor, dull, practical fool can never be made to see that the theoretical and the abstract outvalue in mere almighty dollars all his stupid practical ashes of sense.

Our way goes, with ups and downs, till now we are skirting the foot of the Great Smoky range along Big Creek. As we passed a vine-covered cottage this morning, just after four fingers of inspiration out of the canteen, Blanc said: "Panier, I know why the frugal Frenchman, with his dread of owing anybody anything, drinks wine instead of water."

"Why?" asked Panier, unsuspiciously.

"Because he'd eau for water."

An awful silence fell upon the Wagonauts. After consulting the canteen and brooding for a time in solemn silence, Panier retorted: "The pun's as thin as the fluid."

"O, you're not acqua-ainted with the fluid last mentioned," replied the unconquerable Blanc.

"Wat-er dreadful mental condition you're in," replied Panier.

"Udor'n't understand it," came back Blanc, resorting to the Greek for water; "I can make a wasser one than that if I try." This is the sort of thing I've to endure as best I may. Blanc is now engaged on his life work, "A Plan for the Improvement of the Punning

Capacities of the English Language, with an Introduction by Max Müller."

At last, wet inside and out, tired, soggy, muddy, looking like a draggled game cock of a rainy evening, we came to Big Creek bridge and Hopkin's farm at the foot of Great Smoky and five miles from the summit of Mount Sterling Gap.

"Let 'em have the corn; we can buy it back," said a kind-faced woman. I'm sure she was looking at me; Blanc thinks she was gazing at him; Panier is sure that a glance at his shad-like form aroused her sympathies, and his quixotic appearance perhaps justified the belief. After lunch it rained as it only rains in these mountains. As Virgil justly says, "All Jove came down." We found dry spots in the leaky cabin, which the proprietor doesn't mend as respects the roof, because he's going to move some time or other; and, because, like the house of the Arkansas Traveler, it doesn't leak when it's dry, and he can't work on it when it's raining.

After lunch Mrs. Hopkins, the mother of our hostess, came in in a melting mood—a woman of sixty-five, with coal black hair, form erect, and straight as an arrow; face still good-looking and step as springy as at eighteen, with a trace of lingering widow coquetry, a deal of good sense, and such dry humor as I observed once in Mrs. Clemens, the good old mother of "Mark Twain." Her husband had been killed as a Union man during the bitterness of civil war in East Tennessee, but she showed no trace of bitterness when told that we had been on the other side. On the contrary, she displayed a hospitable womanly interest. Asking my name—as the best-looking of the Wagonauts—she said: "Any kin to Dr. Doak, the Presbyterian teacher and preacher? I reckon everybody in East Tennessee knows them. All the 'ristocrats was Presbyterians. There was the Brazzletons and the Inmans. I lived in Jefferson County before we moved here. Them Inmans was good folks and the boys was good boys." She was surprised to hear that John H. Inman was a New York millionaire. Blanc vows that I said "Yes, we were all Presbyterians," when the old lady said that all the Presbyterians were aristocrats; but I didn't.

John H. Inman is worthy a word in passing—a man for Tennessee and the South to be not only proud of, but grateful to. Born at Dandridge, East Tennessee, he left a bank clerkship at the beginning of the war, to enlist as a private in a Confederate regiment, whence, through his superior business talents, he was promoted in a few weeks to be orderly sergeant, the business man of the company—indeed, of the regiment. He served faithfully in the ranks, a mark for every bullet, until his business and organizing capacity called for his services in the quarter-master's department, where he spent the last two years of the war, surrendering in North Carolina a division quarter-master. Certainly a rapid rise for a youth of seventeen!

Returning to his home in East Tennessee, he found fortune swept away, fields ravaged, houses burned, negroes gone, and a spirit of hatred and jealousy, which makes life unendurable. Indeed, life was not possible, except to one too weak, or unknown, to attract attention. Like thousands of the best intellect and energy of East Tennessee, he went, driven from his home by that insane spirit, which enriched communities north, south, east, and west, with the intellect and enterprise of men who have made leading citizens everywhere, and left East Tennessee to languish to this day, as France suffered from the exile of the Huguenots, and Germany from the banishment of the Palatinates. East Tennessee is naturally the most favored of lands, but it is only just beginning to recover from the injustice which gave Georgia so many citizens and scattered so many far and wide to be foremost in the great Southern strides forward.

Mr. Inman went to New York, friendless and penniless, and toiled for three years as clerk in a cotton house, becoming a partner at the end of that time. In 1888 the house of Inman & Swan was the absolute ruler of the American cotton market, with a widespread and powerful influence upon the markets of the world. In 1888 he began to turn his attention to railroading, and afterwards became President of the Richmond and Danville Railroad Company. Perhaps no man in America has an equal intellectual grasp of the railroad situation of the South. He has made no mistakes.

Devoted to the South and its people, he has done more than any one man to help on that material development which has advanced the South beyond its former glory and wealth and given it a glimpse of power, glory, and riches, of which the world has had no example—a progress due, and due almost entirely, to its own sons and to their grasp of its possibilities. Like many another East Tennessean, such as Lowrie in commerce, and Campbell Wallace in railroading, he has found his chief, although not entire field, in Georgia and the Virginia and North Carolina sea-board. Such a Southern worker, too, is John W. Thomas, the able President of the N., C., and St. L. Railway. Although only about forty, he has made a fortune which is estimated at $5,000,000.

His services to his native land and, broader than that, to all of his country are enhanced by the fact that he not only can cherish honorable memories of determined and gallant service in the great, honorable, and unparalleled struggle of the South, and equally patriotic services to the South in the restoration of its wasted resources; but he is besides, what is worth more than all, a genial, kind, charitable, and affable Christian gentleman, a consistent member of the Presbyterian Church, and every way worthy of the honor paid to him North and South.

By this time the mother had slipped into her daughter's best dry gown and sat swinging her feet, quite jauntily for sixty-five. By way of recompense for our intrusion, the canteen was passed. The daughter tossed off about five fingers, remarking: "'Tain't often I see any whisky; but I like it. I think its healthy." A drink that would have appalled any of our party didn't seem to affect her in the slightest. The old lady looked slily at her daughter: "Jinny got copperhead bit and like to a died five year ago, an' I don't b'lieve she'll ever git over likin' a drop o' liquor for that old snake bite." The old lady surrounded no inconsiderable dram herself by way of preparation for future snake bites.

A pretty mountain maiden of about sixteen now came in, carrying a two-bushel bag of corn, followed by a big, lazy lout of a brother, carrying his own carcass and looking rather overburdened with that. The girl was a model for a sculptor in limb and torso.

Begging permission to occupy the stable for the night, our hostess said we could stay in the back room, which she assured us didn't leak much. With one chair, the bed, and a keg, we were soon comfortably installed.

These people are capitalists for this country. The wife seemed to be the head of the house and the owner of things generally. They had sold off a stock of goods, some cattle and land, and were awaiting collections before removing to the Red Banks of Nola Chuckee, Unicoi County. Our hostess was a kind, good woman, into whose sound mind had come gleams of a higher civilization than she enjoyed. Barefooted, with gown at half leg, she was magnificently formed, bust and limb, and carried herself, head erect, with unconscious pride. She had been beautiful before child-bearing; hard work and the loss of an older child had written hard lines in her face. She was still handsome, especially when talking. In repose her mouth dropped into harsh angles. Sensible, easy, and fluent, using good English, with a quiet, occasional flash of humor and appreciation of our obscurest puns, she was evidently superior to her lazy husband.

It was as good as a comedy to see a little girl of nine or ten, when she came in from school, gaze for the first time upon a real African. Aristarchus blushed as she scanned his coal black features with childish awe. "How did the missionary get so black?" she asked. Her mother explained that the only negro ever seen in this cove in her day came preaching through the country as a Missionary Baptist and preached at an old schoolhouse. He was an object of curiosity and was finally ridden on a rail and given notice to quit. Since that time traditions of a black missionary have lingered in the valley. The little girl inquired again: "What does the missionary cut his hair so short for?"

Strange as this may appear, it is simple fact. The mountaineer prejudice against the negro is insurmountable; hence the African rarely ventures into these valleys, though he is in no danger as a servant and is treated as an equal so long as he avoids trying to live here.

During the afternoon Blanc strolled, gum-coated, down the road. A half hour after a native with a red petticoat about his shoulders, called for me to say that a gentleman at the bridge wanted to see me about a "deer drive." "Gracious; in this rain? What has got into Blanc?" Donning a gum coat, I went with him to the bridge; and there I witnessed a sight for all nine of the Muses: Blanc, sitting upon the low parapet of the bridge, in the drizzling rain, notebook in hand, writing an ode to Big Creek.

"What did you come for? I sent that idiot off to get rid of him. Clear out and don't interrupt me. This is the finest thing I ever saw."

The scene was well worthy of the praise

bestowed. The broad, clear Big Creek came dashing down, with many a fall and cascade and many a long, deep reach or clear pool, literally out of the clouds. A quarter of a mile above, the low white mist lay upon the surface of the water, contrasting with, as it partly rose and mingled with, the dark spruce boughs. The river seemed to burst, like an escaped prisoner, out of its covert of cloud and dark green. On it comes, yonder leaping ten feet down into a deep pool, yonder cascading over great granite blocks for a stretch of fifty yards, then down over a hundred feet of smooth stone, and then with a sweep under the low bridge. Below the bridge it swept majestically around a curve between meadows and cornfield, to be lost downstream in the mists again. Add to this scene, genius at work in the very throes of parturition, in a gum coat, with Faber No. 2 and a notebook. I left him in labor over a bi-syllabic synonym to rhyme with "river." I suggested "shiver," and hastened back to the fire.

Half an hour later Blanc came straggling

in, a most bedraggled and forlorn-looking spectacle. He said that he had not succeeded as well with his poem as he had wished; that it was not up to his usual standard; "but," he added with characteristic modesty, "it's better poetry than either of you can write." As proof of his assertion, he made profert of several rain-spattered pages from a notebook, whereupon was inscribed his effusion. For the benefit of posterity it is here transcribed under the title given it by the author:

A Pluvial Dithyramb.

Like Goldsmith's lone and lonely traveller,
  "Remote, unfriended, melancholy, slow,"
Far from the madding crowd's annoying stir,
  While rolls the restless river far below,
I sit upon this damp old bridge and think
How very much I'd like to have a drink!

Not from the river—such a draught, indeed,
  Were far too frigid for my cold condition;
Saint Paul himself did not extend, we read,
  To stomach-medicine his prohibition—
And so vouchsafe, O Ceres, from thy bounty,
A generous *quantum suf.* of Lincoln county! *

---

* The name of a favorite brand of Tennessee whisky.

So near and yet so far! the blue smoke curls
    Above the humble cabin where, anon,
Heedless of me, my friends—the caitiff churls!—
    Will pull the corncob from the demijohn,
And, as they guzzle there in godless glee,
Will leave the world to dryness and to me!

Dryness within—'tis wet enough without:
    Much like the "Ancient Mariner," I think,
I find there's water, water all about,
    And not a drop of anything to drink;
Great wind-blown sheets of rain fill all the sky,
The stream is full—*eheu!* so am not I!

And here I sit, Marius-like, amid
    The ruins of this Carthaginian bridge,
Wooing the Muse, who still keeps coyly hid
    Among the pines and other trees indig-
Enous to her fuliginous retreat—
I hope Marius had a drier seat!

The air is full of sound: the cataract's roar,
    The sullen sough of wind through dripping trees;
And o'er it all I hear distinct, once more,
    The raucous voice of Alcibiades *
The old, familiar query skyward toss,
Asking: "Am I a soljer ov de cross?"

I came to write a poem for the maid
    Whose large and generous welcome was so sweet—

---

* One of the very classical names given our colored driver.

A grateful sonnet, erewhile to be laid
    In homage at her large and generous feet,
Magenta-stockinged--but the hope is vain:
How can a man write verses in the rain?
Here goes once more: O beauteous mountain maid!
    O dryad, naiad, nymph, rolled into one,
Sporting like "Amaryllis in the shade,"
    Or glancing 'twixt the sunshine and the sun,
In gay, glad, giddy, girlsome glee—alack!
There goes a large, cold raindrop down my back!

"Dryad," said I? Nay, anything but them!
    I call to mind the Carolina sages
Whose luminous, omniscient apothegm
    Will gild with glory all the coming ages,
And make without disguise the frank admission:
I really could not stand a dry-ad-dition!

Is life worth living longer? There, below,
    The river rages, all athirst for blood;
Dare I, despite its cruel-gleaming flow,
    Leap, Cassius-like, into this angry flood,
And be "a dem'd, damp, moist, unpleasant body?"
Not now—I think I'll go and try to find a toddy!

Describing the scene to Panier, our hostess said: "Is he a poet, a real poet?" We assured her that he was a great poet. He modestly declined to read his verses to her; but we detected him giving her a revised copy substantially like that given above. Panier gave her four pretty lines which cost him two hours' labor, inscribed to her little daughter. I saw myself fading into obscurity. "Madam," I said, "these gentlemen have to cudgel their dull brains as if they were oxen only to drag out a few lines of poor verse. I'll go back home if I can't talk better poetry than they can write. Here goes to your beautiful Big Creek:

>Big Creek arose
>From her couch of snows
>In the far blue Al'ghany Mountains;
>From cloud and from crag,
>With many a jag"—

"Hold on there," shouted the mean, envious Panier and Blanc in disgraceful chorus, "you played that game the time you had that 'jag' over on the Roan."

Without noticing the mean interruption, I proceeded:

>And gliding and springing,
>Big Creek went singing,
>In murmurs as soft as sleep.
>The earth seemed to love her,
>And heaven smiled above her,
>As she lingered toward the deep.

Our fair hostess clapped her hands with delight: "Ah, I know that's real poetry; I never heard anything like that." Panier and Blanc meanly charged me with stealing those beautiful lines; but the charge fell flat, and I shall linger in the traditions of this valley as the genuine poet of Big Creek.

We turned sharply up the mountain side; and, after a mile of winding, our last night's resting place lay almost straight down beneath us. In this pure atmosphere walking scarcely tires the toiler; but one would like the option of riding when one has hired a team. It was as much as Sysyphus, the driver, and Frank could do to pull Jim and the wagon. Soon it grew misty and no rainfall was needed to saturate our garments. Now and then the mists were all swept aside by some magical zephyr, disclosing beautiful views of height on height, peak on peak above and lovely valleys below, glistening with raindrops in the moment's sunlight. Floating clouds lie spread out like fleeces of enchanted wool, or lazily climb the mountain sides, or, deep down in the valleys, long white lines of mist mark out the winding ways of devious creeks, or fill whole valleys with fairy lakes, dark in the shadows, and brightly gleaming in the chance sunlight.

Here, at a turn in the road, a lovely cloud view opens up to the left and rear. A dozen distant lofty peaks and lower mountains stand amphitheatre-like, dim grey-blue in the thin clouds, like ghosts of departed mountains revisiting the scene of former sentinel duty. The upper clouds drift away, the mists grow white and clear, the blue deepens upon mountain sides and summits, the wind rapidly scatters the mist in whirling sprays, curling upward and away, until the unveiled blue of mountains looks into the azure vault above. In the distance between high peaks are seen the far-off Chilhowies, with their low sandstone-girt sides and pine-crowned sharp ridges. A half mile on and all is dark again; the rain comes down in torrents and Jupiter Pluvius drags closer his rubber blanket.

We are now in the region of the metamorphic rocks, which, for the most part, lie in North Carolina. The vegetation has become alpine and we are rapidly approaching the climate and flora of Canada. Animal life there is almost none. No hum or chirp of humble bee, honey bee, dragon fly, or cricket enlivens the way. Save now and then the scream of the eagle, the cawing of a crow, or the croak of a raven, no sound is ever heard upon these remote summits.

All human sounds have been left far below, the hush is burdensome, and the soughing of the wind but makes the silence oppressively audible. In this awful stillness we welcome the voice of the glorious thunder, "leaping the live crags among," reëchoing from peak to peak and crag to crag, shaking the very granite foundations beneath us. In the midst of the gloom of Erebus we are gladdened by the fierce lightning, flashing lurid and zigzag, sharply piercing the pale mists with lambent tongues of fire, weaving plexures of flame through and through black thunder clouds, broadly inspiring and lighting up the whole vast enveloping cloud mass around us.

At last we draw nigh to Mount Sterling

Gap, on the divide, at the summit of the great Appalachian chain. The valleys and mountains of Tennessee lie behind us. We are about to enter a new-old country, inhabited by a similar, but not by the same, people, dwelling upon a geological foundation of an older series, with a different flora. The people of the slopes behind us were mostly Union people, now Republicans. Retaining most of their primitive characteristics, they have been a little more in contact with the world than their Carolina brethren over the great divide. The forms of speech differ slightly. In the main, the same people without close connections with one another have developed subtle differences easier to note than to describe or define.

The Carolina people here were mostly Southern and are now generally Democrats. This difference, however, was due to political conditions. Beyond this there are surface, not radical, differences such as peoples develop when dwelling apart, each secluded from the great world and that association which makes the cultivated classes in all civilized countries so much of one type that it is hard to assign the nationality of photographic selections from the educated classes of different nations.

The reader may expect a treatise on dialect. Much of my boyhood was spent hunting, fishing, and frolicking with these people. I have since visited the mountain regions of North Carolina and Tennessee a great deal, observing closely the manners, customs, and speech of the people. I can easily trace such peculiarities of speech as I have observed to the days of Chaucer, Sir Thomas More, and Mandeville, but I have heard no dialect. Romance writers have not been able to resist the temptation to surprise their readers with most uncolloquial dialect, which lies chiefly in their own grotesque spelling. Such dialect is as easily read by a cultivated student as a page of the Hamlet quarto of 1603, or the folio of 1623, with their variegated spelling and antique letters. We have here simply the language of tradition, without the growth of written speech. These people have had their antique language handed down to them from father to son. Hence it has responded slowly to the changes going on amongst the lettered classes. It is still plain English speech, as easily understood when spoken as the talk of the Harvard graduate. I have known a dialect monger to put into the mouth of a mountain character the Yankee "heft" for "weight," or "guess" for "reckon;" when it may be assumed that the man who uses either "heft" or "guess" was either in the Federal army or of the household of one who was.

But here's Mount Sterling Gap, and a good-natured looking fellow waiting astride the fence, of whom we would ask some questions about our road; so that the further journeyings of the Wagonauts are reserved for the next chapter—after we've tapped the canteen. So "here's to you unt your vam'-lies; unt may they live long unt prosper."

CHAPTER IV.

"Ef I lived in a groun' hog hole, I'd fight for it."
(A Patriot.)

THE rain and fog shut off the fine views from Mount Sterling, so that the reader is spared any description of them. Upon the high peaks above the gap we could catch glimpses of spruces and firs. These conifers belong to the latitude of Canada, and are found here at altitudes of 5,000 and 6,000 feet respectively. The fir yields balsam in what are called "balsam blisters" on the trunk. But for these "blisters" the inexperienced eye could scarcely tell the fir from the spruce. In grasshopper season these summits are frequented by the pheasant and wild turkey; but generally they are left to the eagle and the raven. The soil is fertile, but too cold to produce anything valuable except grasses and the hellebore. The continual condensation supplies numerous cold springs and provides a trout stream for every little vale.

The region we are about to enter, and that to the west and south of us, is the wildest, most interesting, and least visited of all the mountainous country east of the Mississippi. One or two peaks of the Black in the Blue Ridge, two hundred miles east and north, are perhaps higher than any hereabout; but for number of high peaks, vastness of mountain masses, wildness and grandeur this region excels.

In the beauty of its streams, such as the Big and Little Pigeon, the Little Tennessee, the Cataloochee, the Tuskeseegee, the Ocona-Luftee, and the Socoah and Jonathan's Creek, it far surpasses any region I have ever visited. In cultivated lands, broad valleys, and level reaches it is surpassed by the valleys of the Nola Chuckee, but the pasturage here is the finest I have ever seen. The owners of these wild lands may fence them, pay taxes, and "range" their own cattle thereon, but any citizen may graze lands unfenced, rent free. The mineral and timber resources are first rate and both comparatively untouched. Iron, silver, gold, lead, graphite, granite, and many other minerals are found in workable quantities; and mineral and timber agents and capitalists seeking investments are beginning to "prospect."

Wet and dripping from a passing shower, the Wagonauts waited in "Starling Gap" while Aquarius and Frank hauled Jim up the steep slope. Getting in and lighting our pipes, we hailed the man on the fence—the only native we've met who was on the fence—the natives are generally very positive. He was a good man—a man to tie to—he'd been to get a basket of apples for his mother-in-law. Panier took advantage of the "gap," separating him from his domestic establishment to indulge in profane jests upon the mother-in-law, which I have severely suppressed, although he has since furnished them to me carefully written out, but meanly credited to Blanc, whom I'm not going to get into trouble.

The three miles down the mountain to Lizard Spring were soon made, and here we halted for luncheon and respects to the canteen. Making another ascent, we descended into the valley of the Cataloochee and stopped for the night at Fayette Palmer's. The Cataloochee is a noted and a beautiful trout stream. This Dolly Varden, dainty minnow, as Blanc scornfully calls him, seeks the pure cold waters of the higher streams after the month of June, where the water is overarched with spruce, pine, and laurel and kept cold, where huckleberries come dancing down the waves and the flies are sweet and cool. It was too late for fly fishing, and we had in native parlance to "sink for 'em." We'd soon a fine string apiece, and Pisces was set to cleaning the catch while I donned my white apron and got out the olive oil. Mindful of my last experience of mountain cooking of trout, I entrusted myself with the culinary operations.

The pompano stands next to the trout in delicacy of flavor and firmness of flesh; but the speckled trout, born in the clouds, nurtured in the mists—"children of the mist"—whose home is in the coldest and purest brooks, whose dainty food is the finest berries and the delicatest flies and moths, is the finest of all the fish. The epicure scorns sauce with its dainty pink flesh, melting like butter in the mouth.

Blanc, who came out "loaded for bar," came in not entirely gameless, and perhaps saved two valuable lives by shooting a genuine copperhead. This serpent abounds in these valleys. While not so venomous as the rattlesnake, it makes up for venom in vigor of attack and the certainty of its aim. I have known many people bitten by both reptiles, but I have never known death to result from the bite of either. With two kegs of snake antidote, we felt snake-proof. Weary with clambering over rocks, and drowsy from the effects of our drenching, we tapped the canteen, smoked one pipe of ravishing tobacco, and were lulled to sleep by the musical murmurings of the bright Cataloochee. By morning Panier and I were off—up the slopes of the Great Smoky, with bait and rods, eager for a great catch; but the heavy rains had so swollen the Cataloochee that our prospect of sport had faded. We could not wait for the uncertain clearing of the river, and Ferguson was ordered to take the road.

Upon a high clearing on the divide between Cataloochee and Jonathan's Creek we met a divinely ugly native, with a strong but pleasant face, a keen eye, eyebrows like a moustache, and a genuine moustache sprouting upon the end of his huge red nose.

"You-uns from South Calliner?" he hailed, as we drove up.

"Nashville, Tennessee."

"Min'rals er timber?" he asked.

Every party of tourists is subjected to rigid scrutiny, and suspected of being prospectors for minerals or timber, or United States officers ferreting out moonshiners. I have deemed it unnecessary to mention my connection with the government; for, while I would scorn to use information gathered while on a pleasure tour, it might prove dangerous to be suspected. The natives are as jealous of mine and timber hunters as of those who interfere with their right to make their own fire-water.

"They allus carries fishing tackle," he said, when we showed him our sporting outfit. He didn't believe a word we said. "The 'revenues' allus does that," he said. At last he said he'd like to show us some "speciments" he'd gathered. They were fine specimens of iron pyrites, which we assured him might have a future value.

The mountain man is always between the horns of a dreadful dilemma, fearing that some prospector may "bag" a good thing "onbeknowns" to the native; or that he may himself fail to "bag" a good thing by neglecting to use deftly the superior knowledge of the prospecting outsider.

Crossing the clearing, we stopped to enjoy the fine views. The sun was shining brightly; the few floating clouds hung high in the heavens, and a dark rain cloud clinging to the highest peaks of the Great Smoky in our rear rather enhanced than marred the prospect. To our left rear lay the lofty peak of Mount Sterling. In the west, mountain mass lay piled upon mountain mass, above which towered Quoi-Ahna-Catoosa, serene in the clear sunlight, and heavily timbered down into the basin at its foot.

On the other side the view lies almost appalling in its grandeur of infinite distances, mountain masses, broad basins, long, trough-like valleys, farms and fields, high up on mountain slopes, as far as the eye can reach, to the dim, misty crests of far ranges in Georgia and South Carolina. At our feet lies the pretty vale of Jonathan's Creek, dotted with farmhouses and checkered with field and woodland, with here and there the curling smoke of human habitations, up to the thick forests upon the slopes and summits of Socoah, up which the eye wanders to the Gap, through which our road will carry us to-morrow, into the Indian country.

Southward Waynesville nestles in a broad plain, surrounded by its amphitheatrical mountain ranges. Further around to the east yawn the canyons of the French Broad, lying darksome in the shadows of Paint Mountain, near Warm Springs. In the far distance to the southeast towers Pisgah Peak, one of the tallest of the Appalachian system. East, a little southerly, stand the great mountains about Asheville. This is the furthest, wildest, and every way finest mountain view we have had.

While we were gazing, our native gave us necessary information. Something brought up the war. "Were you in it?" I said.

"Stranger, I were," he replied, with a hurt expression.

If he looked hurt by an implied doubt as to whether he'd been to the big wars that make ambition virtue, his expression was both hurt and wrathful when I asked him which side he was on.

"Ef I lived in a groun' hog hole, I'd fight fur it," he replied.

"Where did you serve?" asked Blanc.

"I were with Ransom, in ole Virginny," he answered, with modest pride.

"Then you saw some fighting. Get hurt?" asked Blanc.

"Half this hand," he said, holding up a maimed hand. "I were thar nigh to the eend—in the hospital at Petersburg. I were shot purty nigh the last, an' bar'ly git out afore the Yankee line lapped round our boys ez we got out'n Petersburg."

His picturesque and finely expressed "Ef I lived in a groun' hog hole, I'd fight for it" told the whole duty of a man to the people he lives with and to the country he lives in. "Let's take a bumper to Ransom and the tar-heels," said Panier, drawing out the canteen. "Stranger, I reckon you know this kind of bottle?"

The veteran's eye gleamed. "Got one like 'er down home," said he. "Got one of 'em at Big Bethel, and carried her clean through —regular Yankee cantlet. A Yankee bullet give her a cut at the Wilderness, an' a piece o' shell dinted her some at Petersburg, when we fit at the 'crater;' but I've got her her yit."

He poured out a modest six fingers, gazed afar, as if memory were lit up with battle heights, flaming crests of well-charged hills and cherished recollections of camp, field, and comrade; and then, with a start and a long breath, he said: "Well, here's to you-uns and yourn. We done nothin' to be ashamed of. We han't done nothin' after all; but we worried 'em. I han't got nothin' agin nobody; I han't got nothin' to take back, nuther."

The Confederacy had no better troops than these same "Tar-heels," who walked on their toes to the front and stuck their tarred heels into the ground on their retreat. Nothing was more enjoyed than our meeting with this simple-minded veteran, whose strong face and rude but eloquent talk showed plain sense and magnanimity.

With a hearty shake of the hand at parting, we turned down the slope toward Jonathan's Creek. At a store and a mill by the way we found about thirty natives assembled to hear a trial for assault and battery. The defendant had escaped, and Hamlet was being played in Hamlet's absence. A native unfortunately let it out that a meeting of Confederate veterans was to be held on the heels of the trial, and we had much trouble getting Blanc to forego this opportunity to make a speech. Blanc is utterly lacking in sportsmanlike pride. He disgraced us here by buying from an urchin a fine string of trout, caught in Jonathan's Creek.

Where the sign board read, "Waynesville, 5 miles," we turned up the creek, and came to a new white church and schoolhouse. It is a good traveling rule to be the more circumspect the further you go from home. Panier wanted to take possession, but Blanc and I went to a neighboring house and asked for the key. The old man was obdurate. My statement that we were Christian gentlemen from Nashville went for naught. I inquired about the denomination of the church, determined to work Blanc's pious face for all it was worth as a deacon or ruling elder. It was a union church of all Christians. I was puzzled. "What is your persuasion?" I asked.

The old man was a Baptist.

"Do you think that Christ would have turned off a stranger with a horse that was born tired?" I asked.

"They hold me responsible," he replied.

"Would any of the disciples—even Judas —have turned three weary travelers, with a worn-out horse and far from home, out into all out-doors, with a storm brewing? denied them shelter, and driven them out into the cold world?"

A happy thought struck me. "By the way, stranger, do Baptists ever take a little for their stomachs' sake and their often infirmities?"

The pious disciple cast out a chew of tobacco as big as a dumpling, and made a long and minute inquiry into the astronomy of the waning moon. As the last gurgle died on the ear I added: "Do you remember the blsesed promise of the Scriptures: 'Inasmuch as ye did it unto one of these, ye did it unto me.'"

"I reckon I'll haf to let you in," said he.

Our camping at Jonathan's church perhaps saved some child's life. Serpentarius was removing a plank which lay in the way of the wagon, when Blanc, with his keen eye for snakes, and remarkable capacity for adapting it to frequent calls for the canteen, spied a copperhead coiled and ready for business, and blew him to Orcus. Blanc is largely ahead on snakes, this being his fourth copperhead, besides five water moccasins. He sees more snakes than the rest of the Wagonauts, and hence kills more.

This is a lovely valley, cut centrally by a beautiful stream. The fertile soil is well cultivated and the vale thickly settled and dotted with neat, comfortable houses—double log and frame; and, remote as are these wilds, many people of education, thought, and of some travel and cultivation, dwell here, and would not live elsewhere if the world were given them. The fences are good, living is cheap, and the people live well—if plenty is well. Their cooking is execrable. It would make Delmonico weep, and Brillat-Savarin commit suicide.

We have not encountered the mean log and mud hovel of many parts of North Carolina, with daubed chimney, ash hopper, pig pen, three-gourd martin box on a pole, and big wash kettle with "battlin' stick," and dozens of tow-headed children, and an old woman in front dipping snuff.

Kupferkopf could scarcely be induced to

feed, after the copperhead incident. I cooked our disgraceful string of purchased trout, Panier made coffee, and Blanc cut and spread the spruce boughs and ferns in the church. After a delicious supper and a pipeful of B. F. Gravely, we turned the sacred edifice into a dormitory, and slept soundly to the tuneful voices of Jonathan's Creek, except that we were once aroused by Blanc's visions of snakes and calling for the canteen of antidote; and once again by Panier's complaining of jabberwocks in the chimney and of a class of schoolgirl fleas engaged in calisthenic exercises down the small of his back.

After a delightful plunge in the creek and a gorgeous breakfast, we swept and cleaned up the church for Sunday school, and set out for Socoah Gap and Qualla Reservation. Ot-o-no os-te-nau-lee us-ke-baw, ve-ra-ci-us ta-le-stori Ram-pe is reserved for the next chapter.

CHAPTER V.

In the afternoon they came into a land
Where it seemed always afternoon.
All round the coast the languid air did swoon,
Full-faced above the valley stood the moon,
And, like a downward smoke, the slender stream
Along the cliff to fall and pause and fall did seem.
        (Tennyson.)

SOCOAH is a high mountain range, with a broad low gap, through which our road runs into sleepy, Rip-Van-Winkle Qualla Reservation. The road winds by the side of Jonathan's Creek, up one of the wildest gorges I have ever steered a wheeled conveyance through. Sometimes it is a broad, moist, cool vale, with slight incline, covered with dense forests of all kinds of trees, with trunks all moss-covered in that moist air. Again it is a deep, rocky gorge, where the road winds through dense laurel thickets, beneath whose dark shadows the creek roars and foams with never a glimpse of the sun even at noonday.

The soil is very fertile and vegetation luxuriant, with fine pasturage. These gorges—the haunts of wolves, bears, and wild cats—run up to the heights of Socoah, to the eye one mass of laurel, hemlock, and ivy, contrasted with gray, lichen-covered granites, with alternately clear-sweeping and white-foaming waters, gleaming through the green and the gray.

The road was but one degree removed from the impracticable. At one point it required work, and I turned myself into a sapper and miner; and, for my pains, had my foot rolled upon and bruised by a huge rock. No chance to ride, pain or no pain. It required the united efforts of our party, with Xenophon leading the team, to lift Jim and the wagon up the steep, rocky way, assisted by a kindly mountaineer. At last one steep incline, through thickets of impervious laurel, and we are in Socoah Gap, on the line of Qualla Cherokee Reservation. After a half hour of water cure below a cold spring, Dr. Blanc applied a moist tobacco leaf to my wounds; so that I suffered but little more with it, although it was already badly swollen and black from extravasated blood. Tobacco applied in time is almost a preventive of tetanus from rusty iron wounds and curative of all bruises.

Here, upon the edge of Qualla, in Socoah Gap, looking down upon the wigwams of the red man, and contemplating the land of the aborigines, we expected to see some wild savage burst with war whoop and tomahawk out of the forest. Instead of that, a well-dressed gentleman rode up to the cattle fence, which encloses a few acres of pasture in the Gap, and saluted in moderate English. His skin was red, but otherwise he was quite modern and civil. He even rejoiced in a plain North Carolina title, and was known as Col. James Hornblower, although generally called for short Jim Hornblower. Jim is a well to do Cherokee, who lives three miles down the Socoah from the Gap. I was moved to interview Col. Hornblower on the subject of corn for our team. At first he had no corn; then he couldn't sell any.

In 1830, Col. Drowning Bear, a good Indian, saw that fire water was shipping his people off to the happy hunting grounds. He began a temperance movement which speedily worked a great reform and cured the whole tribe of bibulation. The authentic history of North Carolina says that this reform has continued down to this day. I have a great respect for history. With a scientific view and certain base notions concerning corn, I drew out the canteen and carelessly remarked: "Hi-po-no lence ke-na-pe so-to-naus-tee, Col. Hornblower." Whether it was the taking military title, the smiling, inviting appearance of the canteen, or the pleasure of finding a paleface who could speak good Cherokee, I don't know. Any way Col. James Hornblower embraced the canteen and looked up at the sun to see what time it was, shading his eyes with the canteen. "Six bells, Colonel," I said; "go ahead." He went ahead on both engines. "O-co-co ex-haustee, Col. Hornblower," I said; "Go-to-no-mo-stop." Still he gazed at the sun. "Pete—Bob—Jack," I exclaimed, and I set it down in my notebook that the reform of Mr. Drowning Bear had not lasted down to these modern times, or at least had not embraced Col. James Hornblower.

When the red man seemed to be duly mellowed, I delicately mentioned the subject of corn in good Cherokee: "So-me maize, Indi-an corn, heap selle, big chief Hornblower." "Ugh, ugh, come down right way—big heap bushel, seventy-five cents." I thought it was fixed, but the paleface isn't always, by a canteenful, as smart as he thinks himself, when he's dealing with the wily red man.

The views from Socoah are fine, but interrupted by timber. The valleys of the Indian country lie below us in the early light—

With ærial softness clad
And beautiful with morning's purple beams.

Why is it that so few poets have sung the beauties of mountain scenery? Is it because they are remote from human life, which, after all, is the poet's highest theme? Are the thoughts that arise, the sentiments that swell in the soul, too vast for utterance by souls that know best how inadequate is all expression? Old ocean has been sung in all her moods. Byron has touched the thunder storms of Jura in lines as beautiful as the storm. In Manfred, in close connection with human sentiment and action, he has depicted briefly the glories of Alpine scenery. Wordsworth is almost the only poet who has sung in continued strain the mountains and their varying moods. He sings as if they had spoken to him and he had understood. They must speak some message to all well-attuned souls.

The Wagonauts are out enjoying a quiet tourist life, with jest and song and easy philosophy and thorough, but not profound, enjoyment of beauty. To drink the draught of nature to the depths one must go, as Scott says, to view aright fair Melrose, "go alone, the while."

One may stand alone on yonder blue dome, or upon the "bald, blear skull" of yonder high-placed crag, with no sound save the rippling of the trickling rill, as it starts down the mountain side on its way to the eternal sea, or the whisperings of the winds—the lenes sussurri—as it speaks to the firs and spruces—spirit sounds, voices of the mountain—far from the reach of all human sounds of kindred men, above all the sounds of creatures and things ruled by man—neigh of horse, bleat of lambs, low of heifer, crow of cock, chirp of familiar bird or insect—and feel, like Manfred, face to face, with solemn, silent nature; or, like the "Wanderer," in the "Excursion," when that dark mountain spirit, the man-shunning raven, comes hoarsely croaking and flapping his black Plutonian wings athwart the scene:

> If the solitary nightingale be mute;
> And the soft woodlark here did never chaunt
> Her vespers, nature fails not to provide
> Impulse and utterance. The whispering air
> Sends inspiration from the shadowy heights
> And blind recesses of the caverned rocks;
> The little rills and caverns numberless,
> Inaudible by daylight, blend their notes
> With the loud streams; and after, at the hour
> When issue forth the first pale stars, is heard,
> Within the circle of their fabric huge,
> One voice—the solitary raven, flying
> Athwart the concave of the dark blue dome,
> Unseen, perchance above all power of sight—
> An iron knell.

I confess to a late-grown fondness for a sort of free and easy comrade communing with nature; but there are some "secret, sweet, and precious" delights—some profound and ravishing mysteries, which may not be shared, which will only impart a fee-joy "due to some single soul." But one worshipper at a time may be initiated within nature's inmost shrines.

Setting out with the promise of Col. James Hornblower to meet us at his wigwam below, we began the steep descent of Socoah. "Alas, poor Lo," I thought as I gazed upon these sterile, thinly clad lands, with grim irony bestowed upon these aborigines, for services rendered the early settlers, and upon the fertile paleface lands upon the other side of Socoah Gap, "he gets the worst of every bargain." It's always: "I'll take the turkey and you take the crow; or you take the crow and I'll take the turkey," and "Ugh! paleface never say turkey to Injun onct."

Our road runs steeply down Socoah Creek, which has already become a considerable stream as it comes down from the upper peaks of the Socoah. A mile and a half down the broad stream roars, foaming down a deep, rocky canyon, arched with laurels, fringed with ivies, and overhung with dark hemlock boughs, wet and sparkling with continual spray. The gorge is lined with vast broken, jagged, craggy cliffs, and the creek makes its toilsome way over and among huge granites of many tons' weight, piled in wild confusion in its channel.

At a turn in the road we come upon the magnificent Socoah Falls. The bold crystal stream dashes, with a long sweep, twenty feet down a smooth incline, out of a dark covert of green boughs into the sunlight, falling checkered through sparse overhanging boughs, and pauses on the brink for the first wild leap for liberty, "frenetic to be free." Foaming and boiling on the edge of a deep chasm,

> Between walls
> Of shadowy granite in a gleaming pass,

it plunges down twenty feet into a bubbling cauldron; gathers strength and, a few feet farther on, leaps into the abyss below—

> Through wavering lights and shadows broke,
> Rolling, a slumberous sheet of foam below.

Thence out of the sunlight and out of its swirling basin it glides, sending up thin clouds of steamy spray, touched by the slant morning sunbeams to all the rainbow hues, and goes gliding into the deep shadows of dark granites and darker spruce boughs, to roll and tumble and fret and fume, over, under, around, and over great boulders, here and there disclosing, through green boughs, ravishing views of nature's wild magnificence.

Here, in the Indian country, one may imagine some dusky Alfriata, spirit of some blue Juniata, wooed by dusky lover, in unison with the swelling notes of this wildly and weirdly tuneful waterfall—forest notes, suited to nature's wildest mood—where civilized lovers would seek purling brooks and softer music.

According to the only tradition I have found lingering here, the last battle fought by the Cherokees of this region was fought here in Socoah Gap. Strangely this was a conflict between rival Cherokees. Of wars

SOCOAH FALLS.

with the paleface they have no tradition left. A little learning has banished tradition and oral transmission. The name of John Sevier has been forgot, while the names of rival Indian heroes of a far distant day still linger in shadowy form. It was near here, if not here, that "Nola Chuckee Jack" burst into the Indian country, spread death, ruin, and dismay, and escaped by another route when his way was blocked by all but one tall peak. The tradition of the last fight runs that a band of Cherokees from the coast came by Socoah, seeking the West. They were met in this gap, ambuscaded near the falls, and but one spared, to be sent disgracefully back to tell his tribe to send more men, and no more squaws.

Reaching the comfortable home and well-tilled farm of Jim Hornblower, we waited for that wily red man, whom we had seen fifty yards behind us not a half mile back. James came not. Dusky children appeared at the doors, and then vanished. We invaded Jim's wigwam. No Jim, no squaw, no papoose. We knocked and yelled. No reply, no corn.

Sadly, wiser, and with profounder knowledge of the red man, we went on.

The sociable paleface builds his cabin near the road; the solitary red man, wrapped in the mantle of his own solitude and silence, builds the road as far from all springs as he can, and then builds his house by the spring. As we went on down the valley a wild, shrill halloo came from behind, and was caught up and went reëchoing down the valley before us. Strange! The houses were all closed. A deathlike stillness reigned. No answer. Inhospitable! Scipio Africanus expresses himself as favorable to an early retreat; but we came to see the Indians, and we're going through somehow. We know that the great Father's paleface children are as safe here as at their own firesides. It is merely Indian surliness and suspicion. Their white borderers have told us, over on the other side of the line, that there is not a country on earth freer from violence, theft, or crime. The fields are filled with oats in neat stacks, and hay in cocks. The lands a mile or so below the summit of the Gap are very fertile, and the houses and fences are good. The agriculture is generally as good as that of the white mountaineers who dwell skirting the reservation. We meet a party of bucks and squaws going to Warm Springs to play a game of ball. The squaws—*Der Frauen Zustand ist beklagenswerth*—carry the burdens, bats, bows and arrows. They beg tobacco and accept whisky, and tell us we can get corn—heap, plenty corn—but we don't, and we can't.

At last we come to a house by the roadside—double-log, well-built, with long front porch. An old Bashi-Bazouk, with tremendous moustache and the general appearance of a Turk, bushy, white eyebrows and eagle eye, sat upon the floor, surrounded by four squaws. We hailed him: "Bashi-Bazouk, have you any corn?"

"Ugh! ugh!"

"Colonel, sell us a bushel; horse about to drop."

"Got no corn."

The old reprobate! One of the squaws was all the time pointing to her mouth, intimating that they needed the corn to eat. They eyed us curiously, suspiciously—not hostilely. The squaws and papooses spoke Cherokee to one another, and all the while they could speak as good English as we could.

The red devils would drink our whisky, chew our tobacco, and make any sort of promise of corn from the next house. From the only white storekeeper dwelling among them we afterward learned that if they were starving and had an abundance to sell, and were anxious to sell, they wouldn't sell a grain of corn to a stranger. Finally we stopped, dug up the hatchet, danced a war dance, smoked a war pipe, poured a libation out of the keg, and passed a resolution:

Resolved, That Lo loveth not his paleface brother; that Lo deserves his sad fate; that sympathy with Lo is misplaced and mawkish; that, after all the Great Father has done for Lo during the past two hundred years, Lo is an ingrate; that Lo has never been hit a lick amiss; that we hope somebody will hit Lo again; that there is no good Indian but a dead Indian.

Then, in desperation, Panier and I resolved

to risk, if need be to sacrifice, Blanc to the general weal. The vote stood: Affirmative: Ramp, 10; Panier, 2; Xerxes, 1; Frank, 9-10; Jim, 1-10. Total, 14 votes. Negative: Blanc, 1. Carried, *nem. con.* Much against his will, Panier and I painted Blanc a fine yellow with pigment ochre from our canvased beef, blacked his eyebrows with powder, and hid his auricomous poll beneath a slouch hat. He was a noble red man when we got through with him and admonished him: "Go, Young-man-afraid-his-horse-will-die, get us corn, if you have to dig up the hatchet, raise the war whoop, scalp and slay."

We provided him with wampum for peaceful barter, and saw him off. With dismal face Blanc laid down the fence, and steered himself through the gap to a distant cabin which seemed to promise maize. After awaiting for many minutes the result of our desperate expedient, we heard a wild war whoop, a trampling as if a herd of buffalo had been stampeded, a tearing noise and a rending asunder of bushes, and Blanc burst upon our astonished gaze, making 2:10 out of the laurel into the open ground. He looked like a pair of shears, opened to full stretch, as his legs encompassed at one bound a bit of open ground. His fiery red head gleamed upon the view for a moment like a meteor or a red fire beacon or a will-o'-the-wisp, as if

> The sun had sent him, like a ray,
> To say that he was coming up that way.

And he plunged into the thicket again like an extinguished farthing-dip. Behind him came four bucks, tomahawks and scalping knives in hand, in full cry, war whoop and all, followed by five squaws and fourteen of the younger fry, all head up, opening on Blanc's trail. Panier and I took a tree apiece, sending Picketus Africanus out to scout. Panier had a shotgun and two pistols; I was armed with two thirty-eights, with the schnicker schnee stuck in my belt.

In a moment Blanc rushed out of the thicket again, trailing after him about two hundred yards of muscadine vines and other climbing plants whose botanical character I didn't have time to observe, his clothes torn, his neck and hands scratched by briers and

BLANC ON THE WARPATH.

brambles, the perspiration streaking the yellow ochre and powder stains down his face in rare and beautiful combinations; so that his "human face divine" looked like a cross-barred gridiron or a miniature of the Madrid Escurial, while his fiery eyes glared over the rubiginous point of his rubicund nose. His skullcap was off, and his knotted and combined locks stood on end, each particular hair a burning and a shining light.

"Where's the corn?" I said calmly, determined to soothe the distracted nerves of the Wagonauts, and to put on a bold front before the arrival of the enemy.

"Corn, h—ll!" he shouted. "Look at those autochthonal, aboriginal, ferro-rubiginous devils." Blanc swears fearfully classic and dreadfully polyglot oaths when he's excited.

As the redskins burst out of the laurel, with war whoop, tomahawk, and scalping knife, we covered them with our guns. They slowed down, paused, halted, grew silent. *Conticuere omnes.*

"Wait for the word," I whispered, as

calmly as if I'd been buttering a muffin, beginning coolly to sharpen the fall schnicker-schnee upon the trunk of a great scaly bark hickory tree, striking fire at every stroke, feeling the edge, glancing calmly at the sharp edge and at the astonished redskins, and seeming to make a mental note of the number and character of the scalps that would adorn my wampum belt and delight the warlike souls of our happy papooses when we returned home to our wigwams from the warpath.

I never felt more bloodthirsty. Scalpetus Africanus now came in from a successful scout, and retired to the rear. Blanc here disgraced himself by wanting to go off and establish a hospital and put up a yellow flag as the surgeon of the Wagonauts.

I could see the light of battle and the Berserker rage of his Teutonic ancestors blazing in the bloodshot eye of Panier. I gave the enemy a significant glance, and brought the schnicker-schnee one more wipe down the great trunk of the scaly bark. It gave out a ring that resounded far up and down the sides of old Socoah, and struck out a blaze of wild fire that illumined the forests far and near. The redskins stole off with a disappointed "Ugh! ugh!" I have observed that all well-regulated Indians "Ugh! ugh!" in Cooper's and other border novels.

The remaining chapters of this part of my thrilling narrative may be found continued in the *New York Ledger*.

The corn problem was really serious. It isn't right to steal, but we made up our minds that we were going to have oats or corn.

It is the holy Sabbath day. We come now to a wild gorge, tributary to the Socoah, which sparkles with promise of trout. A friendly Indian, before whose eyes we waved the canteen, told us that it contained "heap trout." It being six bells, we tied up on account of the holy Sabbath, merciful to our beasts, and needing Sabbatic rest ourselves. Then we didn't wet a line, or have two hours of good fly fishing up three miles of creek, rich in the speckled beauties; or catch fifty trout, and regale ourselves with a regal meal, cooked by a fire kindled in an old hickory stump. I've no doubt but that we could have done it if it hadn't been Sunday. As it was Sunday, we didn't wet a line. Honest.

Moving on from our resting place, we began to meet more and more Indians in Sunday dress, the squaws with a very decided fancy for red, the bucks in ordinary store clothes, and very good clothes, too. Panier and Blanc bitterly complained of me that I exchanged my sombre tie for a cravat of fiery red, as we entered the reservation. It made them deeply envious to see the young squaws of female persuasion gaze at me with admiring eyes.

We stopped and talked to most of the redskins, the men usually talking as a preface to requests for tobacco, and then shutting up like clams and relapsing into Cherokee. The young men were reticent, except when the canteen was brought out. The squaws affected to be ignorant of English, and wouldn't talk at all. Not even my flaming necktie would draw them out. I think this was on account of Blanc and Panier, for they generally gazed at me with mute admiration.

The natives had been to service, held by David Crow, a native preacher.

At last we came to about fifty braves at a creek crossing, engaged in conversation before separating for their homes. As they stood jabbering Cherokee by the roadside, I addressed one portly fellow, who looked like a man in authority. He told us that corn was scarce, but that oats were abundant, and we should have feed. He directed a young buck to go with us, and furnish oats. Our taciturn friend tapped the canteen vigorously, and finally brought us to both oats and corn. It was time, for Jim lay down at this point and declined to make further effort; so that we had to send Jehu Africanus on Frank to bring back the corn. He left us with a look which said plainly: "When you see me again, this scalp lock of mine will be dangling at some wild brave's wampum belt." Ootsie-tootsie sent back the corn and oats, and came himself to see how James and the canteen were getting on.

Taking advantage of our rest to plunge into the creek, we were surprised by a bevy of dusky maidens; but they didn't seem to be at all surprised.

After feeding and rest we were able to move on over the round, well-timbered hills of the beautiful Ocona-Luftee, a shallow, but broad, clear, lovely stream, far more beautiful than the famed "blue Juniata" of Campbell. Our crossing is in full view of Yellow Hills, the capital of Qualla Reservation, a vile American name substituted for the beautiful Indian name of Qualla. It is a picturesque village, set in amongst high hills, with neat cottages and large, convenient school buildings and store houses extended along the banks of the Ocona-Luftee. The large white house of the Superintendent sits upon a lovely knoll, where the United States flag is flying. Further up and higher is the residence of the Chief of the Qualla branch of the Cherokee tribe, Col. N. J. Smith.

As we cross the river a long line of Indian boys and girls files over a high foot log from a Sunday jaunt upon the lofty hill overlooking the village. As we draw near all faces

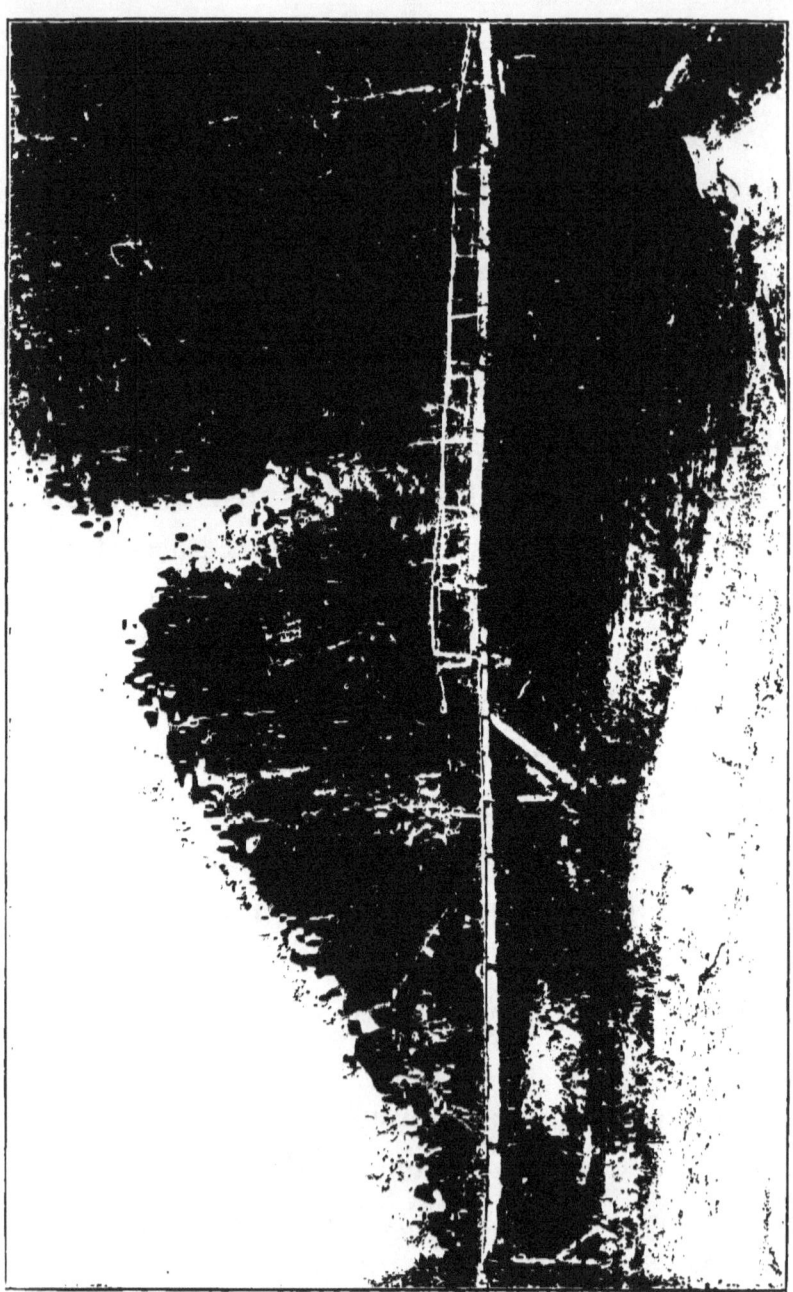

OCONA-LUFTEE.

wear signs of growing culture, satisfaction, and happiness.

I reserve for the next chapter some account of this rarely visited, quaint, and curious bit of barbarism and slowly dissipating savagery, set here in the midst of civilization—a mere speck upon the vast country east of the Mississippi, a lost atom, so insignificant that few people have ever heard or know that there is a Cherokee settlement and a tribe dwelling in North Carolina.

(224)

CHAPTER VI.

Lo, the poor Indian. (Pope.)

I WAS puzzled how to smuggle this chapter in under my rule. The information is valuable, but, perhaps, not useful. If it were useful, the world would have to suffer. Since it contains information it shall be cut short. Brevity's the soul of wit, where utility is the essence of stupidity. It's a crying pity that the useful should have been invented to make life not worth the living and to fill the world with stupid people, so muddy and dull of brain and so slow of foot that all the good things, such as money and money's worth, actually run over them on the road and fill their pockets. The Greeks, pretty well for their day, illustrated this with the story of the slow tortoise winning the race over the swift-footed hare—only the race should have overtaken the tortoise, actually run over him and forced him to win it, while the hare

CHIEF N.J. SMITH.

should have "got left" by his own very swiftness.

In 1806, when Georgia had determined that her civilized Cherokees should leave their happy homes, fertile fields, and fruitful orchards, where they were happier, peacefuller, and, in some respects, more civilized than their white neighbors, who coveted their lands; and the national government had adopted the removal policy, a division of opinion occurred amongst the North Carolina Cherokees. The State of North Carolina, the justest of all the colonies in its dealings with its aborigines, was willing, because of services rendered the infant colony, to allow them to stay. Part went and part stayed. Qualla Reservation—known to the Indians as Qualla Division, or the Eastern Division of Indian Territory—was set apart for those who stayed.

In 1830 the Qualla people had become besotted, drunken, and vile, while the Indian Territory branch, afar from the white man and fire water, had prospered and grown rich and civilized. Drowning Bear, a man of power and character, devoted himself to the reform of his people. It is true that most of these Indians will drink when liquor is offered, but the reform was genuine and lasting. Race sentiment and opinion is against liquors, and the laws against selling liquors to Indians are easily enforced.

The only really dark blot upon the paleface treatment of the aborigines was this deportation of the Georgia Cherokees, because they alone of all the Indians had made genuine and thorough progress in civilization. The Cherokees seem to stand like the Caucasian among the races, the only Indian tribe that has exhibited a fitness for anything but to be made give place to those who will use and not cumber the ground.

The war, which enlisted most of them in the Confederate service, chiefly in Thomas's Cherokee Legion, and among them Col. N. J. Smith, the present Chief, interrupted their progress at Qualla. Thomas became insane and lost most of the money belonging to the Cherokees, and is now in the North Carolina Asylum for the Insane. Material losses were of small consequence. War itself did not disturb them, for no Federal force ever entered the Cherokee country; but the demoralization of war affected them as it did others and them partly by affecting others.

Some years ago the Qualla Cherokees were willing to migrate, and in 1870 about two hundred did go to Indian Territory. They are now willing to remain here, although individuals from time to time seek the main tribe, and there is at all times close communication, and singly and in small parties they pass back and forth between Qualla and Tahlequah.

Here they vote, exercise all rights of citizenship, including having a slice of their Reservation annually sold off by the State for taxes. Whether they are citizens by prescription or by statute I do not know.

Their position is peculiar. The Reservation is held in some sort of guardianship by the United States, and the United States Government exercises police powers, interdicts sales of liquors, and provides for their education. The right of eminent domain is actually in the State of North Carolina. The Cherokees elect a Council and a Chief every four years. The lands are held in common, with a repartitioning every few years, with provision for equitable allowance for betterments and equalization of poor with fertile lands. The white storekeeper told me that they never engage in barter now. They buy and sell for cash or on credit, and pay their debts. Many of them are thrifty and accumulating.

Until within a few years they voted the Democratic ticket. During the Blaine and Logan canvass, on account of Gen. Logan's Indian descent, most of the Cherokee vote was cast for the Republican ticket. In the election of 1888 they defeated the Democratic candidate for Congress, but he was a man they would not vote for. The Democrats charge this state of affairs upon the "Friends," who have sole charge of the education of the Qualla Indians. The Friends have not done well since, and they have been accused of mismanagement. The Superintendent, especially, is accused by the Chief of stirring up dissensions. The Chief, N. J. Smith, is a staunch Democrat. During Mr. Cleveland's administration an effort was made to substitute some other educational care, but the Indiana Friends alone could be induced to undertake the task, and they were finally reinstated.

In 1850 there were seven hundred Cherokees in Qualla, including a few Delawares and Catawbas, divided into seven clans, with seven towns. There are now about twelve or fifteen hundred, and Yellow Hills has been substituted for Qualla as the capital.

The mission is conducted on the farming-out plan, the government paying $12,000 a year and furnishing the farm lands, the vineyards, gardens, and ample school buildings. Yellow Hills is a beautiful village, neat, orderly, and picturesque. There is an air of sobriety and order which indicates energy and an executive brain. The satisfied, studious look of the pupils, male and female, in about equal proportions, is a touching spectacle when one reflects upon the sad and yet inevitable history and lot of this unfortunate race and considers that but a meagre remnant seems now about to redeem the past, after the crime of savagery has been expiated and the race has almost expired under the inexorable law of nature which makes climbing bitterly hard and seemingly cruel.

That portion of the corn crop which we carry in our kegs gives us no trouble; but there is no end of trouble with that part of last year's crop which we can't get. Jim is unable to move beyond Yellow Hills. There is no corn at the store, and the Superintendent is out driving. Leaving Blanc absorbed in a thrilling border novel, Panier and I visited the school, where we saw about a hundred well-formed, handsome Indian maidens, mostly of decidedly mixed blood, although we were told that only a small percentage was of mixed blood. Three of those we saw were of unmistakable African descent. From the schoolhouse we went to call upon the Chief, Col. N. J. Smith, whom we found talking on his front porch with a gentleman to whom he introduced us as his son-in-law from Indian Territory. The chief invited us to be seated, and conversed affably for an hour. He is a robust man of about fifty, decidedly handsome in feature, with coal-black ringlets pomaded down his shoulders, keen black eyes, large, well-formed nose and high cheek bones. Well dressed in a neat business suit, he displayed a becoming, but not offensive or excessive, self-appreciation. Erect and commanding in form, he must have been a striking figure in full Confederate uniform on horseback, as he is now as a dignified gentleman. He is not only a gentleman in appearance but in manners, and he writes a beautiful hand and spells perfectly.

Asked about the position of the Cherokees, he said they were amenable to the civil and criminal laws of North Carolina. "But," he added, "we generally try to settle all differences and disputes in Council and usually succeed." Reticent and silent as the Indian usually is, he admitted that the Council in session is about as unruly a body as the Lower House of the American Congress. I spoke of two Indian comrades, the Walking-Stick brothers, with whom I had served during the late war.

"O yes; Walking-Stick, Ot-on-a-ul-a-na-us-tee. The older Ot-on-a-ul-a-na-us-tee is dead, but I will have the other here in the morning if you can stay."

The Walking-Stick Freres were not in demand as messmates in my regiment; but a drunken fellow, named Jake Doyle, who had once been a brilliant young lawyer, who was himself uncurrent as a messmate, took them in and formed a mess. The redskins adorned the back and sides of their tent with various picture-writings of the battles they never fought, descriptive of days and nights on the warpath after Yankee scalps, which were never scalped. Jake inscribed the front of the tent with:

"Jake Doyle and Staff."

And reclined at ease and drank all the attainable whiskey, while his Walking-Stick staff did all the work.

Asking the chief about the absence of traditions among his people, he said he had wondered at it; but he could give no explanation of the curious phenomenon. The story of the last battle of the Cherokees at Socoah, with, as he thought, the Catawbas, was the only tradition of which he knew anything at all. A gentleman from Washington was then collecting what he could find concerning their manners, customs, and folklore, and he hoped that he might develop more than he knew himself. Ours was a hasty tour, and of course we attach no importance to what we learned, more than in so far as it coincides with what others have developed concerning the curious loss of all facility in oral transmission. A little learning and a desire for more seems to be the death of traditional learning and legend.

We prefaced all inquiries about the wars of the palefaces and the red men, with the remark that the Cherokees were such magnificent fighters that, if they had had our arms, they might have been the victors. In every case this was received with a broad smile upon faces that seldom smile. Mr. Smith smiled gracefully, bowed proudly, but with a pleased expression, and said: "As we were at home, I think the victory might have remained with us."

The language of the Cherokees is musical and the syllabifications easily caught. Such words as O-to-na-ul-a-na-us-tee, Quo-Ahna-Ca-to-os-a, O-co-na-luf-tee, Na-an-ta-ha-la, Ca-ta-loo-chee, Tenassee, No-la-chuckee and So-co-ah, pronounced Syoko and Tuck-e-see-gee, spoken by them are very musical and the words are easily caught. The language is composed of but few words, and its difficulties lie in its poverty. One word is made to do duty that would be performed by a hundred English words. For instance, the word for a needle stands also for any sharp-pointed instrument. If Tennessee, Nola-Chuckee, Watauga, Holston, Suwanee, and such words were ever Cherokee, they have forgotten them.

The Superintendent kindly supplied us with corn, but was unable to furnish lodgings on account of having a party of United States engineers lodging with him. The store-keeper found us an upper room at the house of the paleface widow with whom he was boarding. Our room was reached by a tumble-down stair, leading up to a ramshackle landing in front of the door, upheld by four posts. The widow's handsome daughter was arranging the room, while we were carrying up our baggage. Blanc and I had made a trip apiece and Panier was making the ascent, with a valise in one hand and the handle of the keg in the other, when the heavy structure gave way and crashed down into the garden. I was looking at Panier's unsteady efforts to steer the keg to where he could tap it "onbeknowns;" but how the stair fell and how Panier made the door-sill, neither he nor I can tell. I'm not surprised that he's ignorant, for reasons I will not mention. When the dust cleared away, the stairs, the landing, the posts, Panier's valise, in sections, and his store of cosmetics were scattered amongst the cabbages, and Panier was clinging to the doorway with one hand, to the keg with the other, and to the bunghole with his teeth. It was a narrow escape from almost certain death.

The widow rushed out, wringing her hands —it was wash day—believing that her daughter had fallen. We tried to relieve her mind

PANIER'S CATASTROPHE.

by pointing to the imprisoned pair, looking out at the door, like a pair of caged turtles, she blushing like a peony and Panier conscious only of the keg's charms. With the aid of Stepachus, Blanc and I soon restored the fallen stairs and relieved the imprisoned pair from their awkward imprisonment.

This accident really happened to Panier, but he meanly came to me as the historiographer of the Wagonautic expedition and said: "That doesn't go." I protested that I'd already half framed it. "If you don't promise to lay it on Blanc, I'll put it in the *Banner* on you." Terrorized and under duress, I made the promise, which I have faithfully redeemed above.

Pisces cleaned the remains of the string of trout which we didn't catch in Socoah on Sunday, and with the addition of basted chicken, roasted eggs, and broiled bacon we made a delightful meal, smoked the pipe of peace, and retired to a sweet sleep on the banks of Ocona-Luftee.

As the sun climbed over the high eastern hills, we bade farewell to the lovely hill-encircled capital of Qualla, to the beautiful Ocona-Luftee, to the fair widow and her fairer daughter, and took the high road over the Tuckeeseegee divide, which narrowly separates Tuckee-see-gee from Ocona-Luftee.

We have gone through the Qualla Cherokee Reservation, down its most populous valley, through its roughest and most picturesque scenery. Coming through, by way of their thoroughfare and by their churches, we have seen most of the population in their Sunday dress and holiday garb, men, women, and children. We have seen their houses and farms and visited them at home, most unwelcome. We have talked to many of them, enjoyed a new and a delightful experience, sauced with some hardships for Jim and some thrilling experiences for Blanc. The curl has been taken out of the knotted and combined locks of Scipio Africanus by abject fear for his scalp, and Blanc's ruby locks have paled to the hue of a farthing tallow candle wick.

In a superficial way we have learned something about Lo, and we think better of him than when corn was scarcer. This Monday morn, we have seen the native at work—the red man, actually at work—driving oxen, reaping, mowing—one actually running a reaper—shade of McCormack! We have passed by and seen a road-working party. Every Indian we have seen this morning has been at work. They are in their work-a-day attire, and even in that they are well dressed.

The ten miles to Charleston, now Bryson City, are soon made, and we are once more in a railroad town, which the Western North Carolina is rapidly connecting with Asheville on one side and Marietta, Ga., on the other. The town is full of prospectors, northern capitalists, mineralogists, and adventurers. A fine hotel has been built, where we found specimens of all sorts of minerals and timber. A company of masons are cutting the fine granites quarried here, with which cheap but ambitious buildings are going up. Panier wanted to camp here because we found at the hotel black coffee, huckleberry pie, and cracked walnuts with silver pickers.

Crossing the Tuckeeseegee over a bridge, we pushed on to the Little Tennessee, by the Nantchala road. We intended to spend a week fishing in the Nantchala, which is a noted trout stream, but Jim has put an end to our sport. We are told that we will have good road down the Little Tennessee and horrible travelling across mountains by the Maryville route; but our informant always comforts us when we tell him we've come by Socoah Gap, with: "Well, ef you-uns is been through the Shoko, you won't see no more bad road."

Of our weary, winding way down the Little Tennessee in the next chapter.

CHAPTER VII.

That night a child might understand
The dev'l had business on his hand.
      (Burns.)

NO corn; a fagged horse. This country has a railroad; but corn is measured in a "half bushel." The people say that the influx of strangers and increased stock-raising have used up last year's crop; but why don't the store-keepers bring corn by rail, instead of buying scant half-bushels, drawn out like coin out of old stockings, by the necessity for a few dimes of cash?

Five miles short of Bushnell, on the railway at the mouth of the Tuckee-see-gee, we had to halt for Jim's convenience. He fell down and declined to assume again the uprightness of a self-respecting equine. Jim's a remarkable animal. He's reduced the art of leaving all the work to his companion to a nicety. He does none of the work and all of the giving up, as if he'd been hard at it.

Frank is also a remarkable animal in his way. Contrary to the usual way, he does all the work and all the blowing. Jim's the only idler I ever saw who didn't blow.

A kind, bustling little woman, with a mingled air of happiness and weariness from toil, made us at home. "Eight children? All yours, madam?" "O yes, and two more—two girls married—one in Kentucky and one in Tennessee." By and by the husband came in from his work: a hale, hearty, blue-eyed man, whom the younger children clambered on, hugged and attacked his pockets. He'd been by the store, for he drew out a paper of candy. He is a renter and fairly well-to-do. Questions are asked, back and forth, and we find that he was with Ransom in Virginia, and was at the battle of the "crater," which he called the "blow up." His graphic private soldier's account of that dreadful slaughter, when the Federals hurled a negro division into an exploded mine and got them slaughtered almost to a man, with small loss, comparatively, to the Confederates, was enjoyed more than one usually enjoys war stories.

The citizen generally doesn't like war tales, because he wasn't there; and the old soldier is generally waiting until he can get his own "yarn" in.

As we fight our battles o'er;
And battles that we never fought before.

A chill fell upon us when he said he was at Petersburg until nigh the wind up. "My brother lost his leg at Petersburg, and I come home."

"Fetched your brother home?" said Panier.

"No; I never fotch him home; he couldn't come; but I knowed I was needed at home, an' I come." The man had clearly been a good soldier. He was evidently a good man, intelligent for his grade, although ignorant and poor. Technically a deserter, the circumstances excused it, if anything can excuse forsaking the cause in which one enlists. Nevertheless, there was a cold lull in the talk; and, when his name was mentioned next day, each one said, by one impulse: "I wish Snider hadn't mentioned his leaving."

For the first time, I tried a bed to-night,

and wished I hadn't. After wrestling with the native burghers of these solitudes wild and inaccesible, I resolved hereafter to try a couch of flax hackles, nettles, chestnut-burrs, thistles, thorns, anything, in preference to a native North Carolina bed of musty straw and dense population.

Our stopping place was named the Willow Fountain—a grave mistake, for it suggested to Blanc to sing; " Tit-willow, tit-willow." A living willow, at the corner of the house, had been bored in the center and was discharging a three inch stream of cold, pure water brought down in a log pipe from a mountain spring a mile above. Aquarius Africanus couldn't be made to understand how a living willow could yield living waters. It stood there to speak for itself, a tree of fifty feet in height, pouring a continual stream of water from a spigot in the trunk, three feet from the ground.

Next morning we crossed the Tuck-ee-see-gee, and pursued our way down the winding trough of the Little Tennessee, whose narrow canyon winds between long, low, steep, thick wooded hills and high bluff knobs, usually with a height of from five to eight hundred feet above the river, with sometimes only room for the road along the brink of the river. Often the road climbs the sides of steep hills, skirting sheer precipices, which rise high above and look down below the road. Sometimes our way winds up to the very summits and then winds down again to avoid some impassable point. This natural Macadam makes Socoah ashamed of itself. Steep and rocky on the hillsides, rocky and dangerous on the cliff edges, we are travelling over the upturned edges of this uphoven stratification, where the whole foundation of the earth is on edge. There are loose rocks, fast rocks, sharp rocks, round rocks, smooth rocks, rugged and ragged rocks, all along the riverside road. It is the worst road on this terrestrial ball, and yet a good engineer and five hundred dollars a mile would make it a good road. Generally North Carolina has the best mountain roads I have ever travelled, especially upon the old thoroughfares of the past, as far west as Mount Sterling; but the impulse didn't last from Raleigh this far west, although this is an old main road.

The season here is further advanced. We were told that the Qualla country is two weeks ahead of the Jonathan's Creek region. Here elder bushes bear dead ripe berries, which were only in bloom on the Cataloochee. The road is lined with two beautiful varieties of wild pea, one lowly, the other high climbing. Many kinds of purple and yellow flowers bloom by the way. I've practiced my botany on Blanc and Panier until it's frazelled to a ravelled edge. Early on our journey I'd no difficulty in convincing them that a field of red clover was, really and botanically a field of white clover, and only red in the botanically unimportant matter of color; whereat they marveled greatly, but swallowed the statement with scientific credulity and unction and made a note of it. Now, names and generalizations drawn from the inner consciousness won't go down any more. I've tried, occasionally, admitting that there are some things I dont know; but this has rather weakened than strengthened the cause.

The river runs, now smooth, now broad, shallow and rippling, now boiling, foaming, and roaring in tumultuous cascades over among and around great granite boulders, now plunging down in long rapids. All along we can see lodged sawlogs among the rocks, log slides on the opposite bank, and great piles of logs, got down too late for the last "tide." The river is muddy with a few inches of rise and it has recently been over our road, which is impassable at high water.

At one point we had to fill up a great hole with rocks before we could go on. Petrea Africanus carelessly threw a great, sharp-edged rock and cut off the toe of Blanc's shoe as clean as if it had been done with a razor. "That's the narrowest escape from an un-toe-ward accident I ever saw," said Panier, unfeelingly. "One foot further, and 'twould have cut off your heel, and you'd have been ill 'heeled' for this road. Indeed, I don't see how you'd have gone toe-ward home, if it had gone an inch further."

Beautiful at first, the scenery of this canyon is a bit monotonous after a few hours' travel, which is a heavy drain on the canteen. There are some lovely scenes and views unexcelled. Here is a magnificent stretch of two miles of calm river, between high, Scotch-looking hills, bounded in the far by lofty mountains which seem to wall in the river and make it a long, silvery lake, high-walled, sylvan, and wild. Below us, seen from the crest of a high hill we've just climbed, lies a heavily wooded island, blue-hued, soft, misty, and lovely in the sunlight—almost a reproduction of a photograph of Loch Katrine and Douglass Island, partly the scene of the "Lady of the Lake." We almost expect, as we gaze, to see Ellen Douglas's light shallop fly across the sparkling waters to meet James-Fitz-James.

Here at this point is a fine contrast. We are climbing up to a level stretch of road along a sheer precipice. We are on the shadowed edge of a hill in a dark forest. The slope above us is one succession of huge rounded rocks, piled in vast confusion toward the summit, and looking down upon us with great round, staring, lichen eyes. Tall trees are growing among the rocks, and here and there wild flowers of all hues mock at adornment of the savage wildness of stupendous rocks, as if sylvan elves had decked the rough head of the mountain in sportive contest, as Titania bedecked the head of Bottom. Scant wild vines clamber over great boulders, and cling to their gray, rugged sides, as they reach, round, massive, and confused, toward the summit, as if Titans had piled here a giant cairn, memorial of some great victory in the Saturnian wars. Beneath us a steep precipice falls into a dense thicket upon the narrow brink of the river, which rushes roaring on between green hills.

Beyond us, in the full sunlight, a green hillside, gently hollowed between two rough ridges, faintly veiled with a pale, filmy blue haze, lies serene and placid over against the dark, rugged, frowning cliff, along whose steep side we are creeping. The sunny sides of the opposite hillside are guarded at ridge edges by sentinel pines, with gray rocks showing through.

As we gaze upon the soft study of mingled light, shadow, and color, we wonder how the painter dares, with his few meager pigments, to attempt such infinity of color, hue, shade, tint, and ever and infinitely varying light effects. And yet it is the artist, after all—not reproducing, but at best merely indicating these effects—who acquaints man with nature, and embodies and interprets its subtle spirit, and brings the soul of man *en rapport* with the soul of nature.

Every minute point upon yonder green hillside has its own hue and tint, its own effects of light and shadow; and yet all is divine unity, chiefly one green of many greens, with here and there gray rock and dusky trunk.

The dark boughs of the spruces furnish the groundwork black, the dark sepia, whence we rise to the warm, bright yellow-green of the box alders. The slaty ash; the bright, green hickories; the dull, green cucumber magnolias; the yellow, light-reflecting chestnuts; the dark-glazed hollies, throwing back the sunbeams; the linns and the various oaks, each with its own peculiar tint; yellow masses of true lovers' knot, woven in golden tapestries at the river's edge; the bright scarlet cones of the flaming sumach; white masses of prickly ash blossoms, showing beneath tangled festoons of wild grape vines which link tree and tree, give infinite variety where there is also perfect unity.

In the center of the sunlit, shallow concave a clustered mass of dark hemlocks gives to our picture its deepest shades. Upon the rocky ridge edges, upon both sides, a thin line of scraggy, yellow-green mountain pines bounds the picture and forms the frame.

Colors, tints, hues, and shades and shadows are as varied as kinds of trees, sorts of rocks, position, angle of light-fall—as varied as there are individual leaves, and as each separate point of the infinity of points in the landscape. The common man can enjoy this; the artist is the man who also knows that he can interpret something of it all to his fellow-man.

A light breeze sweeps over the scene, and instantly upturned leaves, glistening in the sunlight, present a new-blended color mass. The ash and the linn turn up the white underleaves, and everywhere some varying shade of underleaf mingles its hue and tone with upperleaf sides.

A light cloud sweeps across the sky and veils the sun, and all is changed again. Every point and each leaf, each hue in the warm sunlight and the misty, sunlit blue, becomes some new thing in the shadow.

The clouds thicken and the skies darken. The spruces and pines frown grimly and deepen almost to blackness, and the hillside stands lowering over the darkening river. Thunders roar and reverberate along the narrow canyon way; hillside answers hillside with solemn echoes; lightnings flash and light up the Titan cairn above us, gleam upon the long reach of the river below us, and light up the now frowning hill beyond the river, where but now the sunlight sweetly nestled and played.

The rain begins to fall, and all is changed

again. The distant mountains fade from the view; the nigher hills pale into misty indistinctness; and the opposite hill, that was but now so sweet a picture, stands ghostlike in the rain and mist beyond the river. The clouds settle down about us and over us, and our view is confined to the road, the near rocks, the giant trees by the roadside, the towering hemlocks beneath us, and the troubled surface of the dark, rolling river.

It rains in torrents, just when we are obliged to walk up a steep hillside. We hang our coats in the wagon. It's easier drying out woolen shirts than outer clothes, and there are no colds in this air. Scotching, pushing, and sliding we go.

With two feeds of corn and oats, we are independent to-day. We may camp wherever the variable Jim chooses to lie down and "knock off" the work that Frank's doing. There are no houses now along our desolate road—miles and miles of hill and forest, cliff and bluff and mountain, unbroken.

About dusk we come upon a desolate, God-forsaken spot. The very air, miles before we reached it, seemed laden with a foul odor of evil deeds. A suggestion of evil seemed to lurk in the forest by the roadside, as we drew nigh. A spirit of evil seemed to look out of the ruined hewn log house and the surrounding "clearing," as evil glares forth from the faces of wicked men.

> O'er all there hung the shadow of a fear,
>   A sense of mystery the spirit daunted,
> And said as plain as whisper in the ear:
>   The house is haunted.

Foul deeds seemed to have stamped themselves upon the gables, roof-comb, and chimney corners of the ill-browed ruin. Some subtle air of mystery, some uncanny suggestion of dark deeds done here within this lonely cabin, seemed to take shape, and to glower out of crack, cranny, and chimney, as if the shackling tenement were filled with a soul of evil.

There is always some sweet invitation about a human dwelling place. This remote, lonely ruin bore no longer any semblance of the human habitation it had once been. It looked as if some foul fiend—some doing of some foul deed—violating all the laws and rights of human hospitality and fellowship, had instantly blasted it into a seared and scathed dwelling place for the very genius of inhumanity.

Panier, when asked to push through the thick, dank bushes to reconnoitre, drew back instinctively. A weed-grown hell's two-acres of stony ground, that was once a garden, corn patch, and orchard, has not yet been altogether reclaimed by invading forest and thicket, as if forest and thicket yet drew back from the accursed spot. A few larkspurs bloom among the weeds; a sickly marigold and a peony peep out from amongst tall bull nettles, rank nightshades, dense, thick-lipped burdocks, fat docks, and foul-smelling "jimsons." The home-loving plantain has departed from the unholy, unhomelike abode of evil.

The brook that runs out of the thicket glides along with a scared look and a whispered warning, murmuring without music by the corner of the house, as if its sweet voice had been once chilled and its current befouled with some taint that no pure outgushings of cloud or mist or sweet distillations of mica sands had ever been able to wash pure and sweet again.

A few half-rotten peach trees and a scraggy apple tree stand barren of fruit, blasted as by some unfertile curse. A rotting rail, scattered here and there, shows where a fence has separated a perhaps once happy cottage home from the wilderness, which now reaches out its arms to reclaim its own, and yet draws back and shudders to embrace the accursed thing. A pile of rocks, yet one upon another, shows where once outhouses have stood and crumbled with the prevailing curse and its ruin.

Phoibos drove up, with face ashy and hands trembling with fear, and the horses snorted with terror.

As we approach the house a slimy serpent glides beneath the floor, and the wind sighs through the cracks between the logs. The comb of the cabin roof has rotted away, and the rest of the room is leaky; the rafters are damp, discolored, and rotten; the door is gone; the floor has a moist, unwholesome smell, and it has garnered, here and there, wind-blown piles of leaves and filth, which lie rotting in the corners. Horrors! here is a child's doll; and yonder, in a pile of reeking rubbish, is a woman's shoe.

Panicus was eager to drive on, but the Wagonauts are nothing if not brave. We determine to lodge in this dreadful house, though it blast us.

House, "clearing," dying orchard; the dense, gloomy forest; the matted, tangled, impenetrable thickets, which reach up to the very corner of the house; the weed-grown cleared plat, with its mockery of lingering flowers, growing there now as if in awful penance for some unpardonable ancestral sin; the far-stretching wilderness, miles either way to human habitation; the deep, narrow gorge; the sullen, roaring river; the brief piece of road, coming stealthily out of the bushes, and hiding at once in the thicket beyond; the slimy insects, crawling upon the moist rocks of the old, half-fallen chimney, oppress the spirits. One can almost imagine vague forms flitting in the wood, hovering in the dusk of the thicket, peering out of the dark, cavernous recesses whence the timid brook steals upon its fearful way to the dark river.

A mountain-locked lake which the river has formed here lies silent, like a dead sea, mirroring huge, sombre rocks, beyond which the river roars down its rocky channel; and the green, silent, stagnant waters of the lake seem to share the curse of the lonely house, as if a wholesome reach of pure water had been, by one fell curse, dammed here into a silent cesspool.

I confess that I never felt such sickening sinking of the heart as when we found ourselves actually in possession, with our baggage moved in. Something seemed to write in ghostly letters upon the clammy wall: "Who enter here, leave hope behind."

We soon had a bright fire of clapboards burning upon the broken hearth. A bed of glowing coals supplied a supper of broiled breakfast bacon, corned beef, a pot of smoking coffee, and a dozen roasted eggs. After a mere drop to take off the chill of the evening and to clear away the sense of loneliness, we fell to with keen appetites. I'm sure that I've never enjoyed a meal more at the Brunswick.

After supper we spread our beds down—two planks for Blanc, three for Panier and myself—on log ends, off the damp floor, with oilcloths and blankets spread down. The biscuit box, turned on end, serves for a table. Cards are drawn out, and we play " hearts " until we tire of cards, blow out the candles, and fill pipes and smoke and talk—talk low, and whisper of things uncanny and of crimes committed in old houses, of ghosts that walk in lonesome places and haunt old ruins; tell ghost stories, until the hair rises on end, and the chill wind through the open door almost seems to take ghostly form, and the firelight, as it flickers, seems to burn bluer and paler than its wont.

Something chills the fountains of conversation. Talk flags. It is almost midnight. The flickering light of the dying embers casts weird shadows upon the wall. The novel surroundings, our wet garments, and a pipeful more than usual have banished sleep. The deep, monotonous roar of the river beyond the hill sounds ominously solemn and, by contrast, brings to mind the dead-sea lake, whose stagnant waters wash the foot of this accursed patch of ground. Fireflies, like great will-o'-the-wisps, flit uncannily in swamp and thicket, lighting up the scene with a ghostly phosphorescence. The distant howling of wolves is borne in by the wind from the thickets behind us; and it draws nigher and nigher until it resounds uncomfortably close to the open door—that open door which will never shut again. All sounds of katydid, screech owl, night hawk, tree frogs, and the deep bass of the bullfrog in the dead-sea lake below us fill the forest with an uncanny clamor. I have never, even in Southern swamps, heard such fearful chorus of lonesome, awe-inspiring night sounds of insect and night bird, deepening the sense of loneliness and utter desolation.

Panier made a sickly effort to jest about the woman's shoe that lay in the rotting dirt heap in the corner. His words recoiled, and he glanced fearfully around with an involuntary shudder of horror and was silent.

Blanc took the little child's doll as an object about which to weave a ghost story, which made Cowerus shudder and draw himself into the embers; but Blanc only aroused a spirit which would not down. He recoiled, terrified at his own creation, and became silent.

Soon we are all silent, with that silence in which men read one another's thoughts. What crime has cursed this deserted tenement? That some blight lies upon it is certain. Some fatal reputation, stamped upon its features, makes it shunned of men and shuddered at as men steal by—as we shuddered, when foolhardiness tempted us to lodge here.

Does that deepening stain on the floor and the wall, which seems to grow deeper and darker, tell the tale? Anger and the sudden blow? Jealousy and the stealthy axe-stroke and a crushed skull? A guilty pair and a victim sunk in the dark river? Guilt, a sheltered paramour, the stealthy knife, the snake-like gliding toward a darkling couch—a wife blood-boltered and sweltering? There is something.

It is in the air; the walls reek with it; the river's roar shouts it aloud. The wind whispers it with a dying sigh through the pines. The night bird shrieks it out. The brook murmurs it. The screech owl laughs it forth and revels in it. The unwholesome wings of the uncanny bat whisper it as they glide in and out by the open door in the dim firelight.

The firelight is but a faint flickering of dying embers, deepening the shadows in the corners and in the ragged roof, where no friendly star peeps in from on high. We can hear one another's breathings and heart beats.

Something comes gliding in at the open door—something vague, mysteriously taking shape, seeming to diffuse itself and then fading out by all the cracks and crannies of the old cabin. Again it appears, lingers, embodies itself for a moment, and again fades into thin air and vanishes.

Three pistols click and the harsh noise

seems, to our quick senses, to fill all the wild gorge with useless noise. Three voices whisper as one: "Weapons are useless here." It was as a profanation, and yet it was only an instinctive clutching at something.

Whispering together, chilled, and terror-stricken, we agree to speak to it if it return; and the shuddering Panier, the bravest of our party, is appointed to the task.

Again it comes, again takes shape—a vague, misty something—"shape that shape has none"—transparent, but an embodied something, vaguely defined, but defined—a half human shape, with large, flowing drapery, dimly outlined upon the black background of darkness, by the faint flicker of lingering sparks in the fireplace of the huge chimney.

Fear, abject fear—which we do not even conceal from one another—has so keenly sharpened our senses that all sounds, the roar of the river, the dismal sighing of the wind, the howl of the wolf, the cries of night birds, the hoot of the great owl, the screech owl's eldritch laugh—all the solemn, lonely sounds of night and solitude—seem to resound, redoubled, one deep, awful chorus of warning or of mockery.

"What do you seek here?" feebly whispers Panier, our chosen spokesman.

Instantly a commanding and a terrible figure defined itself in the center of the room, reached out a long, bony, white-clad arm and a skeleton, skinny finger; and a voice as sepulchral and deep as if it had come from the earth's profoundest bowels said: "I am thy Governor's ghost. I am the spirit of the Governor of North Carolina. Gentlemen, it's a long time between drinks."

When I awakened at dawn out of a troubled sleep, Panier said: "Ramp, what the devil was the matter with you last night? Blanc and I had got up to tap the canteen—so wet and chilly we couldn't sleep. While we were drinking you fell into the dreadfullest nightmare I ever saw. We couldn't rouse you, and finally we gave you a drink and turned you over to dream it out."

The unmitigated liar! The liars! When they both know as well as I do that we all three saw the ghost of the Governor of North Carolina. It has cured me of lodging in old ruined cabins hereafter. Wise men only need to learn once.

Of our journey to Maryville I will speak in the next chapter.

CHAPTER VIII.

The way was long, the night was cold,
The steeds they were infirm and old.
(Scott.)

WE left the haunted house, glad that it didn't rain during the night, pleased that the Governor of North Carolina paid his respects before we left the State, and glad to get away from a ruin which was only less lonely, forbidding, and desolate in the full morning light than by dusklight. The signboard tells us that it's six miles to Rocky Point. They don't spell well here, and signboard nomenclature would unsettle the old atlases; but they do make signs well in this country. Except at crossroads and forks of the road, where they're especially needed, the roads are well supplied with signboards. Throughout the Indian country we found the mileposts entirely primitive—an arrow pointing the way, with the number of miles notched on the post.

At Rocky Point, where a stony cape narrowed the river, the late rise had lodged a dozen sawlogs in the road, where our way jutted against impassable stones on the far side of a deep creek with an ugly ford. Crossing to where we could leap ashore, we had to spend two hours log rolling. I revived my knowledge of skids, handspikes, "pea," "cut," and "cross-lift;" but I had to confess that Loginus Africanus had more of what is called "judgment" than any of us. Improvising skids and cutting handspikes, we toiled and rolled there in the red-hot sun for almost two hours, until we'd cleared a road by which we could barely pass. Two miles on we met a road-working party, to whom we complained that they hadn't cleared out the obstructions. They looked surprised, and told us they'd been over that part of the road and cut all the overhanging bushes, which was all the law required. It seemed to them excessively funny that they should be expected to move sawlogs, when the next rise would clear them out. We "jawed" at them and they "jawed" back good-natured-ly, and theirs was, truly, the best-humored side of the argument.

As we reach the crest of a long hill, we see Panier start back with horror depicted upon his classic features. Coming up, we see a big rough mountaineer with a hangdog look and a general air of "pure cussedness," holding a long rifle at a recover. When Panier first saw him, he'd a dead bead on him, and he thought his days were numbered; but the fellow was only shooting at a mark set up by the side of the road. "I hain't a gwyne to be a hurtin' uv you-uns," he said. If he had had no gun, we would have advised him to be careful that we didn't hurt him for shooting near to a public highway contrary to law, but we forebore.

This fellow was a fine specimen of the lazy, trifling, do-nothing fellow, that marries a good mountain girl, who must marry somebody—or ought to—and then loafs and lounges, while she toils and slaves and bears him a houseful of children and is his squaw. How they live, He that feedeth the raven—yea, providently caters for the sparrow—only knows. Just beyond him, we come to a cabin, upon a rocky knoll, in a God-forsaken spot, miles from any neighbor habitation, with a bit of garden patch, a few peach trees and cultivable ground nowhere else thereabout.

"Rocky Point, ma'am?" we asked of a pale, thin, but good-looking woman who stood in the doorway nursing a sickly child, with two tow-heads clinging to her apron strings. She wore an air of utter weariness and loneliness, but of meek patience, cow-like rather than human—a woman to be kicked and cuffed and starved, to toil and bear children and go on to the end, because she is of too tough fibre to die, and yet doesn't know what on earth she lives for. Such women, here at least, live to an old age, dry up and die, after years of toil, without knowing that life has imposed upon them more than their share of its burdens.

"Rocky Point, ma'am?"

"Hit air, stranger, an' a rocky p'int hit be, shore enough."

"Spring, ma'am, anywhere hereabout?"

"No, we hain't got any water hyar."

"Lonesome place, ma'am."

"Hit air indeed, stranger; hit's the lonesomest place as ever I lived."

This she said as if the lazy lout who was shooting at the mark there in the "holler" didn't relieve it much of loneliness. Poor devil! she has chosen her lot—to go from cabin to cabin, trudging on foot, moving on, moving on, half starved, all the time toiling, while her lazy husband takes his ease and plays lord and master, until he commits some crime and is gaoled, or gets into some drunken brawl and is killed, and then she weeps and believes she is sorry and makes a better living for her children than he ever made for her.

Three miles now to the summit of Great Smoky—a dreadful road, we've been told. The devil was ne'er so black as he's painted. The road is better than the Socoah road, and far better than the Little Tennessee road, and it isn't a "daisy" either. We have to walk, and it rains; but we toil up, doing the Caledonian—scotching—pushing, slipping, and sliding. Some luxurious people may think that this isn't fun, diversion, enjoyment, but it is.

Coming to a rustic bridge at the foot of a beautiful fall, we defer to a particularly dark cloud, stop and take to the wagon for shelter. A clear, lovely stream here leaps down, by three successive falls, into three successive solid rock basins, landing in a pool of granite, washed clean of sand and gravel, lying, about forty feet in circumference between the bridge and the foot of the cascade. Over the last ledge it falls,

> Descending, disembodied and diffused,
> O'er the smooth surface of an ample crag,
> Lofty and steep and naked as a tower,

Into its broad, clear pool, coming down the the gently inclined face of the smooth, moss-carpeted granite, in a beautiful thin sheet of bubbling water, fifteen feet in width, flanked at either side by foamy, broken, tumultuous streams of greater depth, roaring, cascade-iform, down broken ledges. The clear sheet of water, the smooth ledge, moss-carpeted under the water, the flanking falls five or six feet in width on either side, with their two cascades in their last leap into the pool, formed falls of great beauty.

When the rain ceased, we enjoyed a delicious bath, plunging into the clear, cold basin, leaning reclined against and under the descending sheet of clear water, lying in the troughs of the cascades at the sides and coming out reinvigorated for further climbing.

As we halted in the Great Smoky Gap, three miles from Rocky Point, and upon the divide between Tennessee and North Carolina, the sun was shining brightly. At this high point the valley views in Tennessee, to the Kentucky line, and the mountain views, down to the Georgia and South Carolina lines in North Carolina, are fine and far extended.

To our right towers the regal sunlit head of the Quoi-Ahna-toosa, named from "quoi-ahna," a duck, and "catoosa," a mountain, meaning the "duck-mountain," being covered on its summit with lakes, where ducks pause in their migratory flight. Clingman, an old North Carolina politician, and one Buckley have had quite a quarrel about the Quoi-Ahna-Catoosa. Clingman, when one of the Regents of the Smithsonian Institution, had it named "Clingman's Dome;" while Buckley has had it named for him on some maps. Mapwise it appears both ways. It is a magnificent mountain, perhaps the highest peak east of the Mississippi. Too weighty for the shoulders of either Buckley or Clingman, it should be left alone to bear its own beautiful Indian name.

At this point the Wagonauts barely escaped an insurrection. Blanc drew out his watch and called Panier's attention to the fact that it was 10 o'clock.

"And in an hour it will be 11; and thereby hangs a tale; and thus we ripe and ripe and rot and rot," replied the mixtly Shaksperian Panier.

"A truce to frivolity," replied Blanc. "I propose that we drink to the health of Quoi-Ahna-Catoosa and destruction to all tyrants and an end to this six bells business." Blanc looked really heroic as he concluded his Philippic, and added: " Panier, we've been cheated all the way from Knoxville to this point. We've been in the eastern division, and six bells comes at 10 o'clock by our time. We've been deceived—lost a good hour's drinking every day, cheated of our fair proportion of drinking time by this dissembling despot, whom we've too, far too, long endured. No halfway measures with tyrants. Down with six bells."

Panier is a very bold man; but he's very conservative; law, custom, what's "by ages of possession consecrate" he dares not overturn. I saw from the water in Panier's eye that a half decent excuse would save him.

"Gentlemen," I said, "it's true that I've saved you from yourselves. Invoking established usage, it was not my fault if you lost an hour by failing to set your watches up as you came eastward. Now, I've prepared a little surprise. I've kept hid at the bottom of the mess chest four bottles of real Pomery sec. and no mistake, to be tapped at our last mountain station, homeward bound. Here's the place; there's the wine; there's the spring; and damme if the man who doesn't renew his alliance to the six bells rule, shall have a drop, were he a dessiccated flea, roasting upon Bardolph's nose."

Panier at once took the oath, and Blanc reluctantly followed. In five minutes the Pomery sec. was cooling in a cold mountain-top spring, a rousing fire was burning, the horses were turned loose to graze, and the Wagonauts were resting on the grass, which the rains below had not reached.

Blanc softened as the bubbles and beads of growing coolness gathered upon the graceful taper necks of the champagne bottles and the lizards and frogs crawled lovingly over the glass, wishing they could get in; and he proposed that we should memorialize the Congress of the United States to enact the six bells rule into a law. Exactly at six bells—old time—the canteen was brought out and was tapped by way of priming.

When the sun indicated high noon, Epicurus spread the tablecloth and laid thereon two broiled spring chickens, sundry slices of venison, bought a store, bacon, broiled on the coals, roasted roasting ears, roasted Irish potatoes of the fine mountain kind, beaten biscuits, a pat of butter, a bottle of the finest olives, a bunch of tender lettuce, which has been crisping in the spring, a bunch of water cress, gathered in the valley below, a dozen stuffed hard-boiled eggs, olives stuffed with anchovies, English pickled walnuts, ham sandwiches, a pot of smoking coffee, and four champagne glasses—I had provided the extra one for the absent Brutus—and our spread was ready.

Out of respect for its long and faithful service, the canteen was again tapped, and the hungry Wagonauts fell to with a zest and devoured the edibles with a keen appetite. We had prepared this feast for the gods by judicious purchases along the road; but the champagne was my own provision and a surprise.

We lay on the grass, Roman fashion, "like gods reclined, careless of mankind," making believe that it was Olympus, and we the immortals, regaling ourselves with ambrosia, with nectar a-cooling. When "not the half of our heavy task was done," Ganymede was directed to broach a bottle of champagne from the cooler. As the sparkling nectar bubbled and flashed in the taper glasses, "The Wagonauts" was proposed and drunk, and then the absent Brutus, and then the Quoi-Ahna-Catoosa, to whose sun-crowned head we tipped our glasses. Then Panier proposed Jove; and Blanc proposed Ganymede, Jove's cup-bearer, to which our ebony cup-bearer responded with a grin, as Panier handed him the extra glass.

Never was a meal more delicious or more enjoyed than that regal spread there upon the cool mountain top, where the senses were regaled with the fragrance of wild grape blossoms and of the moist ferns, where the tinkling rill made music fit to accompany a feast of the gods, and the rambling breezes played Æolian strains there under the grateful shadows of spruce and birch.

When all were full, and the last walnut was gone, and the last olive had disappeared, and the last drop of sparkling wine was drained from the goblet, I said: "Gentlemen, I've another little surprise—a pony of *eau de vie*, a *pousse cafe* for the wind-up." Blanc and Panier hugged me, and the rosy cognac was drunk in a health "to the best of caterers, A. T. Ramp," proposed by Blanc, who, with tears in's eyes, distraction in's visage, humbly apologized for his meditated revolt against the six bells rule.

"One more surprise, gentlemen: here are the best of the Henry Clay Perfecto cigars from the Hermitage Club. Let's burn a sweet savor of incense to the spirit of the mountain top." The unimpressible Panier here hugged me, as he lit a fragrant Havana.

At this point the irrepressible and insatiable Panier drew from his pocket a poem. Alcibiades anxiously said he thought we'd "better be gittin' along; mought meet some Injuns in the dark;" but there was no escape. Panier read the following verses:

The Disturbed Mountains.

Like mighty monsters in a vasty lair,
   Aroused to make a fierce protest,
By venturous steps of aliens who dare
   With heedless haste disturb their rest,

The mountains frowned at the invading tread
  Of the Wagonauts, so fresh and free,
Nor less resentful seemed to see them led
  By A. T. Ramp, with schnicker schnee.

And when bold Blanc, athirst for Indian gore,
  With eyes aflame and locks of fire,
Scalped one poor trembling brave, and cried for more,
  They shook their rugged sides with ire.

But Panier, with a gentler art instead,
  By song the mountains did beguile,
Until athwart their frowsy faces spread
  A sun-fetched amplitude of smile.

And when the Brutus read Shakspearean verse,
  In voice so tragical and deep,
The wondering monsters were disarmed of fears,
  And soon were lulled again to sleep.

When he had finished, he waked up Blanc, myself, and Alcibiades, and we toned up our failing systems with a "pony," lit a fresh cigar, and prepared for the road.

We have been told that the descent to the Harding farm is seven miles of good road. The road is good, but the descent seemed to us chiefly ascent. Blanc said that we descended by ascent in order to make a de(s)cent entry into the valley of the Tennessee. The good humor spread over the Wagonaut party by the late dinner enabled this to pass without comment.

At last we came to a tollgate. Tennessee seems to have a monopoly of tollgates upon pikes that exist in the imagination. As it is on the Kentucky border, all turnpikes end at the State line. A traveller by stage from Nashville to Hopkinsville, Ky., one night was suddenly jolted up, bump against the forward part of the coach, as if the world had come to an end. "What the h—ll's the matter, driver?" he shouted.

"Nothin' at all, sir," replied the driver; "jist struck Kaintucky."

A surly young man refused to open the gate until we had paid toll. It was not wise to resist, but we told him that we could no more trust him to open the gate than he could trust us to pay toll. After some altercation, he opened the gate, and we paid the toll. Although the charter, if any ever existed, had been long forfeited, and toll could not be legally collected, the road was good and a public convenience, for which we were willing to pay.

We have now passed through a region of North Carolina unknown to any of our party. I have here seen the mountaineer substantially as I have known him in my youth, when I hunted, fished, danced on puncheon floors, played the fiddle, and enjoyed summer jaunts with him farther to the northeast. In the region that we have passed through he is unchanged by communications and travel. Closer connections have wrought great changes further east; but these have left this region beyond the pale of travel. The country is far more secluded than in earlier days, when great lines of communication ran through this region. Travel has been diverted to rail lines. We did not meet or pass a single vehicle on the Cataloochee road, by Mount Sterling, on the Socoah road, or on the road we are now traveling; and yet these were in the past thoroughfares. Except a few late-come capitalists and prospectors, no strangers have entered here; and the natives, when they do go out, depart by other lines, which are now more convenient. The only actual settlement hereabout was that of a Scotch colony of lumber speculators, and they have failed and gone.

I beg pardon for again referring to dialect. For the chief writer of mountain dialect stories I have a profound respect—for her industry, for her real genius, for works entertaining and worthy in themselves apart from their errors, for her magnificent descriptive powers, although a bit overworked. She seldom uses words not sometimes spoken by the mountain people; but it would take the peculiarities of speech of a thousand to make one character, speaking as her characters do speak. I have never heard the word "hants," or "haunts," in the mountains; although I have heard "hants" among the ignorant people, chiefly the negroes of the lowlands.

The language of these people is as easily understood as that of educated people, and is only singular and outre when written. Written as it is, it would look more unfamiliar than it ever sounds. Besides, she writes most uncolloquial speech; and this is her chief fault. Her characters do not speak, even in their own jargon, as men and women talk. Antique words, although plentiful, do not form the woof and warp of the daily speech of these people. If it were colloquial, her speech would not be their language. This is to violate the truth of fiction; and fiction has its own laws, which will not be violated with impunity.

There is no dialect in this country, unless it be the speech of the French Creoles and of the South Carolina negroes, which is really an unintelligible African jargon. Riley's verses in the speech of the ignorant, the mountain dialect stories, and most of that sort of literature, including the African jargon tales, is mere pestilential cacography. Of all things in literature this is the least worthy. Thackeray's "Yellow Plush Papers" are an instance of a great writer degrading his talents to mere cacography. Both dialect and cacography touch, at their best, merely the outre, the occasional, the transient, and the accidental; where genius seeks the genuine, the true, the lasting, the granite bedrock lines in humanity, which alone can live and be true for all time—to-morrow as to-day, to-day as yesterday. That the lasting may well be fringed and trimmed and decorated with the accidental is true. This the chief writer of mountain stories has done to some extent; but with too much of the outre and accidental, and too little of the permanent and lasting—too much trimming and too little fabric.

This sort of literature has been attractive to Northern readers because it sketches the outre and touches the phases of Southern life about which they are ignorant and of which they seek information; but it cannot form the basis of a lasting literature—not Southern—but depicting Southern life and society as it is and as it was. The coming literature—not of but from the South—descriptive of Southern phases of character, will deal with the broad and eternal lines of social life and character, using the outre and the accidental sparingly, as mere trimmings, local shadings and tinting, laid in upon the broad, the universal, and the permanent.

We are only halfway down the Tennessee side of the Great Smoky when night begins to fall. If we had feed, we could camp anywhere; but Jim must be fed to make Maryville to-morrow. Panier and I walk; Blanc says he scotched, but we remember him as cumbering the wagon. By the time night closed in as black as Erebus, with scarce a star, we were in despair. The road led along deep abysses, and over dangerous hills, and down steep inclines. The sure hand of Lorenzo de Medici is our sole reliance for seeing to-morrow's sun. Lighting a farthing dip, left from our haunted house sojourn, I walked in the center of the road and Lorenzo followed, as well as he could, my guidance. Fortunately, the road was good. My self-sacrifice was loudly applauded; but I really devoted Panier and Blanc to the yawning gulfs on either hand.

About 9 o'clock we reached the Harding farm, and in the dark passed the road which led to the house of Mr. Howard, the present owner. As we drove on down the valley, what I took to be a low-flying meteor whizzed along the ground, on the riverside; and then another and another. "What are they doing with rockets here?" asked Blanc.

"Our coming has been announced; I hope I shall not have to speak to-night in answer to a welcoming address," said Panier.

We halted and hailed a light which shone through the vast river bottom cornfield. We might as well have bayed the moon, for the light was five miles away, so deceptive is eyesight in the night. Our road leads to a gate, which enters a cornfield. We must have missed our way. I blame my eyesight, and I seldom blame myself for any mishap. At least the road may lead to a house. After much winding the road comes to an end, and I get out and light a candle. Searching for the road, I fall into a deep ditch and return to find Blanc and Panier discussing the situation over the canteen. At last I find the road, and we make another mile of interminable cornfield by what turned out next day to be a neighborhood road. Now we're out in the corn again, trampling people's breadstuffs and miring in the soft tilth, until wagon, Wagonauts, horses, and Jehu land in a ditch. We prize out, and halt bewildered.

"We'll sleep here in the wagon," said Blanc. To this Panier agrees and Cerberus applauds. My authority as flag-officer is waning, but I said: "Gentlemen, we will not sleep here." This brings revolt to a head, and I proceed to unfold. "Gentlemen, Wagonauts, our reputation will stand any strain; but if the Knoxville editors hear, as they will, of our being found here at daylight, asleep in a gentleman's cornfield, with a wagon, a driver, and two kegs (chiefly filled with emptiness) and a dry canteen, they will indite such an article as will ruin our reputations; and no man, and what's more no woman, will ever believe that we weren't howling drunk, when we got into that scrape,

> Drunker'n hootin' biled owls,
> Or any other wild fowls.

"There's much truth in that," said Panier.

"I hadn't thought of that," said Blanc.

"Dat's so," remarked the sententious Bacchus Africanus.

"If Blanc's red nose is found where it is usually anchored, near the bunghole, who can receive it other?" I said.

"Who can receive it other?" echoed Panier.

"Who can receive it other?" echoed Blanc.

"Who'll take 'nother?" said Bacchus.

We got out, lifted the wagon around, and drove back toward a house where we saw a light. After two miles of travel it was no nearer than when we started. It was really five miles away across the river; but we did finally come to a light off the road; and, leaving the team, Panier and I went to ask for lodgings. A handsome, robust, neatly dressed woman came to the door, surrounded by a bevy of lovely daughters. Her husband wasn't at home, and they didn't take in strangers. We told her who we were and what was our unfortunate plight, out in the night, far from any house, with worn-out team and a broken axle—an invention of Panier's. Still: "I'm very sorry." A thought struck me. "Madam, have you any water?" As she turned, I said: "Panier, we must show ourselves and trust to her being able to see through our rough attire that we're gentlemen in disguise." We entered the house and the lady was able to know gentlemen disguised. "I'd be sorry to turn gentlemen away at this time of night," she said.

"Shall I have our team driven up to the front, madam," I said, taking it for granted.

"Yes, right there by the gate; the stable is out there; my little boy will show you the way."

In an hour we had surrounded a square meal from our own stores, and were smoking our pipes and laughing at wanton fate cheated, and congratulating our own good luck.

The lady told us that the rockets we had seen were preconcerted signals, arranged between a party of tourists on the mountain top and a house across the river.

And now, last scene of all in this eventful history: after a delicious breakfast with our fair hostess, who dwells at Maryville in the winter for the education of her children, and lives here in the summer and raises flowers and has everything neat and comfortable about her, we are off for the capital of Blount County. It wouldn't have been so bad after all if we had slept in the cornfield; for we were told that the main road here was the neighborhood road which led through the cornfield. We can take a nearer road across Chilhowie range; but we've had enough of Jim in conjunction with mountain roads. We enter the cornfield and pass through many a gate and along the foot of Chilhowie, about twenty miles, to where we pass around the end of the mountain, and across the divide to Maryville. Across the river, as we go, we can see the site of the old Indian settlement, and later paleface fort of Telassee, where was once a large village. The views on the Little Tennessee along here should attract artists from all quarters. I have seen nothing finer or more attractive to the landscape artist than this long, winding trough of the Tennessee and its broad fertile bottoms and vast fields of waving corn, overshadowed by high hills, steep mountains, huge cliffs, and wooded summits.

Out of the mountains, over the foothills of the long sandstone Chilhowie mountain range; and, leaving it in our rear, we stop for lunch and to feed. A grey-eyed mountain damsel—robust, barefooted, good-looking, with an evident policy of her own—comes down to the cool spring and sweet spring house, well stored with milk and butter, to be sold to neighboring watering places; and gives us, for a very modest compensation, fresh, cool buttermilk, delicious sweet milk, and fragrant butter off the clover fields, and made by her own fair hands. She talks pleasantly the while, and with good sense and good English, although she's barefooted. Her father tells us that he's never been ten miles away, although he is a very intelligent man and talks well. He also plays the fiddle, and we have "Rackback Davy," "Old Zip Coon," "Natchez under the Hill," and "Billy in the Lowgrounds." This old-fashioned music moves Panier's not too robust legs to the mazes of the dance.

> Nae cotillons brent new frae France,
> But hornpipes, jigs, strathpeys, an' reels
> Pit life an' mettle in his heels.

He tries "Old Granny" and "Forked Deer;" but "Rickett's Hornpipe" brings out all the grace and mettle in Panier. I stood in amazement, wondering at this Terpsichorean feat, and Blanc lectured him on the undignity of the display there in the "big road." Panier said that the Scriptures recorded that the rams danced and skipped, and lambs hopped, and the hills danced their legs off when the old "chunes" of Zion were played, and he meant to knock it out once more if it blistered his heel.

Blanc had another narrow escape from death here, trying to make what he called a mint julep. He offered the concoction to me, but I suspected treason and poison, and declined. He had violated all julep rules, mashing the leaves up in a cup, when it's the odor and flavor of the mint, and not the taste, that is wanted and prescribed. I recognized the "yerb" at once as a deadly poison.

"Why, it smells like mint," said he.

"O, yes," said I; "you have found a leaf by accident, but most of the plants you've got there are poisonous weeds." I lectured him in good botany, threw out the poisonous "smash," and found him a bunch of real mint.

Our road now lies over long, steep hills, until we reach a beautiful, fertile, but ill-watered country, ten miles from Maryville, with the blue ridge of Chilhowie behind us, stretching, a long sandstone ridge, from near Sevierville southwesterly to the Little Tennessee; and farther, southeastward, tower the far, tall blue peaks of the Great Smoky, in Sevier and Cocke Counties, Tenn.

We are making about a half mile an hour, and are six miles from Maryville, when Jim comes to a dead halt. An old farmer was induced by Panier's persuasive tongue to sell us a feed of corn and oats. Stopping in a long lane, we fed, built a fire by the roadside, and soon had a supper fit for a king, with a pot of fine black coffee, displaying the exquisite touch of Panier in its delicate aroma. I've seldom enjoyed a meal more than that roadside supper. A smoke in the fence corner, and an hour's sleep upon a divan formed of the wagon cushions, and we are off for

Maryville, which we reach about 12 o'clock, finding everybody in bed.

Here I wish to lodge the only complaint I have had to make of Blanc and Panier as traveling companions. I enlivened the dark road with song—operatic gems, ballads, and sentimental verse. My companions have no ear for music. They know not the soothing influences of melody. They've no understanding of the concords of sweet sounds. Their deafness did'nt disturb me in the least. I sang on. I liked it.

The hotel was full; but we secured the soft side of a floor, and, with our blankets, enjoyed a good night's rest, and got up early to view the ancient and picturesque capital of Blount. Maryville is the old seat of a New School Presbyterian Theological Seminary, whence emanated once, from one of its professors, the most remarkable epic poem that was ever composed—a poem now forgot, but deserving revival and such study as Homer has received. I read it in my early days, when my father was a minister of the Old School Church, and procured and enjoyed it as about the kind of doggerel a New School man would write. It is one of the curiosities of literature which deserves embalming. There is a tradition that Payne composed his "Home, Sweet Home" while he was Indian Agent out in this country. That he was such agent is true, but the rest of the tradition is unfounded.

Distrustful of Jim, we bade Saltus Africanus an affectionate good-bye, and left him to wrestle with James and find his way to Knoxville, while we boarded the train. But we were not quite quits with Jim and Jehu. As the train passed by a steep hill we saw Jim stalled fast upon the hillside, and Scipio lashing his side and filling the air with blue blazes of profane speech.

With a very bad horse we have made two hundred and fifty miles of rough mountain road—from Knoxville to Sevierville, and thence around through Qualla, and by the valley of the Little Tennessee, to Maryville and back to Knoxville—a wide circuit.

I humbly apologize to the stricter sort for mention of the keg, which has been really more frequent than its use. Why the convivial has a place in all literature—song, ballad, epic, and romance—I know not; but it has, and I'm not one to fly in the face of established usage. The keg and the canteen were along for use; but their chiefest use has been to point a moral and adorn a tale, with Blanc and Panier as horrible examples.

The good things that have happened I hope I have impartially distributed to Blanc and Panier, only giving myself the worst parts played. I believe that I have not admitted that there is anything I don't know. If I have, I apologize for that.

Having neither hotel nor rail nor river tourists' lines to advertise, I can conscientiously commend the Bald and Roan mountain regions, the wild, picturesque Qualla country, the rugged peaks of the Quoi-Ahna-Catoosa, and the lovely valleys of the Nantehala, the Cataloochee, and the Ocona-Luftee to all tourists of America. To these may be added the equally wild and rugged Asheville country and its beautiful centre city of growing refinement, elegance, and culture, now accessible by rail. In all these regions there is the wildest, noblest, and most picturesque mountain scenery to be found in America this side the Rocky Mountains. I cannot conscientiously advise two kegs; but if I were the tourist, I would not go unprovided with something for the stomach's sake. It's dangerous.

As we entered Knoxville, Achilles drove up to the depot and saluted, borne upon the wings of the wind. In fact, our train had been delayed four hours on the way. Another agonizing parting, and we board the train for Nashville; and the Wagonautic tour of Ramp, Blanc, Panier, and the canteen and two kegs draws to a close, and adjourns *sine die*.

ERRATUM.

The picture of the "moonshiner," Jim, referred to on page 63, was lost too late to supply, and a portrait of another moonshiner, noted in federal courts, is substituted.

(300)

www.ingramcontent.com/pod-product-compliance
Lightning Source LLC
Chambersburg PA
CBHW030821230426
43667CB00008B/1312